THE USES OF PESSIMISM

THE USES OF PESSIMISM

PESSIMISM

And the Danger of False Hope

Roger Scruton

ATLANTIC BOOKS
LONDON

First published in hardback in Great Britain in 2010 by
Atlantic Books, an imprint of Grove Atlantic Ltd.

This paperback edition first published in 2012 by
Atlantic Books, an imprint of Atlantic Books Ltd.

13 15 17 19 20 18 16 14 12

A CIP catalogue record for this book is available
from the British Library.

ISBN: 978 1 84887 201 1
E-Book ISBN: 978 1 84887 881 5

Printed and bound in Great Britain by Clays Ltd, Elcograf S.p.A.

Atlantic Books
An imprint of Atlantic Books Ltd
Ormond House
26–27 Boswell Street
London WC1N 3JZ

Product safety EU representative: Authorised Rep Compliance Ltd., Ground Floor,
71 Lower Baggot Street, Dublin, D02 P593, Ireland. www.arccompliance.com

Contents

Preface

In this book I examine optimism in what Schopenhauer called its
'wicked' or 'unscrupulous' (*bedenkenlos*) form, and show the place
of pessimism in restoring balance and wisdom to the conduct
of human affairs. I don't go along with Schopenhauer's comprehensive gloom, or with the philosophy of renunciation that he
derived from it. I have no doubt that St Paul was right to recommend faith, hope and love (*agape*) as the virtues that order life to
the greater good. But I have no doubt too that hope, detached
from faith and untempered by the evidence of history, is a dangerous asset, and one that threatens not only those who embrace it,
but all those within range of their illusions.

At first, the old myth tells us, the only mortals on earth were
men, to whom Prometheus brought fire in defiance of Zeus.
In revenge Zeus ordered the creation of the first woman, who
was given in marriage to Prometheus's brother. Her name was
Pandora – the all-giving one. And as a wedding gift Zeus gave her

a box, instructing her never to open it. Giving way to her curiosity at last, she opened the box, releasing into the world death, disease, despair, malice, old age, hatred, violence, war and all the other evils that we know. Pandora closed the box at once, and one gift remained inside – the gift of hope: the only remedy, but also the final scourge.

My concern, in the first instance, is with certain fallacies that seem to justify hope, or at least to make disappointment bearable. My examples come from many areas, but they share a common characteristic, which is that they show, at the heart of the unscrupulous optimist's vision, a mistake that is so blindingly obvious that only someone in the grip of self-deception could have overlooked it. It is against this self-deception that pessimism is directed. A study of the uses of pessimism will reveal a most interesting feature of human nature, which is that obvious errors are the hardest to rectify. They may involve mistakes of reasoning; but their cause lies deeper than reason, in emotional needs that will defend themselves with every weapon to hand rather than relinquish the comfort of their easily won illusions. One of my purposes is to trace these emotional needs to their prehistoric source, and to show that civilization is always threatened from below, by patterns of belief and emotion that may once have been useful to our species, but that are useful no longer.

The belief that human beings can either foresee the future or control it to their own advantage ought not to have survived an attentive reading of the *Iliad*, still less of the Old Testament. The fact that it did so is a sober reminder that the argument of this book is entirely futile. You may enjoy it and agree with it, but it will have no influence whatsoever on those whom it calls to account. The irrationalities that I explore are, as the neuronerds put it, 'hard-wired' in the human cortex, and not to be countered by anything so gentle as an argument.

The theme of the collective unreason of mankind is not new, and you might wonder whether there is anything to be added to the great survey that the Scottish poet Charles Mackay published in 1852, entitled *Extraordinary Popular Delusions and the Madness of Crowds*. Mackay's study of prophecies, superstitions, witch-hunts and crusades is a grim reminder that all the things that he sardonically describes have continued in the same frequency and to worse effect since his book was published. Mackay felt that mankind had at last entered a period of scientific knowledge, in which crowds would allow themselves to be corrected by the experts whom previously they had preferred to burn at the stake. Nothing could have been further from the truth. The great crowd movements of communism, Nazism and fascism, in which false hopes were to transform themselves into marching armies, had yet to appear over the horizon. And the rise of the scientific expert did little more than rebrand the witch-hunts and genocides of the twentieth century as rational decisions, for which science had shown the need. The 'liquidation of the kulaks' was justified by 'Marxist science', the racist doctrines of the Nazis were proposed as scientific eugenics, the 'Great Leap Forward' of Mao Zedong was held to be no more than an application of the proven laws of history. Of course the science was phony; but that merely shows that, when unreason triumphs, it does so in the name of reason.

In a more recent study, *Scared to Death*, Christopher Booker and Richard North have examined the panics that have swept across the civilized world in the last two decades. These panics show the other side of unscrupulous optimism: the equally unscrupulous pessimism that comes when false hope is deflated. All of them – from the hysterical belief that two million British people were about to die from the human variant of mad cow disease, to the apocalyptic vision of global warming, from the fear that all the world's computers would shut down at the millennium, to the campaigns against lead in petrol and passive smoking – have been presented as 'science'. And all of them have ignored evidence and argument in favour of a preordained conclusion, accepted because it gives direction and force to a mass movement of the righteous, assembled to cast out the devil from our midst. Those who question or resist are singled out as scapegoats; witch-hunts of the sceptics go hand in hand with adoration of the heroes such as Al Gore who are pointing the way to salvation. And when the panic is over the crowd disperses, having achieved neither relief nor self-knowledge, but merely the readiness for another scare.

In two other recent studies – *How Mumbo-Jumbo Conquered the World* by Francis Wheen, and *Intellectual Impostures* by Alan Sokal and Jean Bricmont – indignant intellectuals have pointed to the ways in which nonsense has taken up residence in the heart of public debate and also in the academy. This nonsense is part of the huge fund of unreason on which the plans and schemes of the optimists draw for their vitality. Nonsense confiscates meaning. It thereby puts truth and falsehood, reason and unreason, light and darkness on an equal footing. It is a blow cast in defence of intellectual freedom, as the optimists construe it, namely the freedom to believe anything at all, provided you feel better for it.

Some of my observations are indeed anticipated by those estimable authors. But my purpose differs from theirs. My theme is less the 'madding crowd' than the scheming individual: the one who, troubled by the imperfect prescriptions contained in custom, common sense and law, looks to another kind of future, in which those old ways of compromise are no longer required. Unscrupulous optimists believe that the difficulties and disorders of humankind can be overcome by some large-scale adjustment: it suffices to devise a new arrangement, a new system, and people will be released from their temporary prison into a realm of success. When it comes to helping others, therefore, all their efforts are put into the abstract scheme for human improvement, and none whatsoever into the personal virtue that might enable them to play the small part that it is given to humans to play in bettering the lot of their fellows. Hope, in their frame of mind, ceases to be a personal virtue, tempering griefs and troubles, teaching patience and sacrifice, and preparing the soul for *agape*. Instead it becomes a mechanism for turning problems into solutions and grief into exultation, without pausing to study the accumulated evidence of human nature, which tells us that the only improvement that lies within our control is the improvement of ourselves.

I have benefited greatly over the years from discussions with Bob Grant, who read an early draft of this book and made many useful criticisms and suggestions. My thanks go also to those who have set an example, by following the rule of *agape*, striving to love people as human beings without hoping that they will turn into something else. I single out Gladys Sweeney and her students at the Institute for the Psychological Sciences, Ian Christie, Jonathan Ruffer, Helena Pechoučková, my sister Elizabeth, and above all my wife Sophie, who has had a particularly hard case to deal with, and yet who still manages to smile.

Sperryville, Virginia, May 2009.

ONE

The First-Person Future

Every scientific advance is welcomed by those who see a use for it, and usually deplored by those who don't. History does not record the protests that surrounded the invention of the wheel. But it certainly records the protests that surrounded the invention of the railways. For the great critic and social philosopher John Ruskin the railways were a ruthless assault on rural tranquillity; they destroyed the sense of place, they uprooted settled communities, they overran the countryside with steel-clad ugliness and urban sprawl. They set us all in motion, when the true point of human life is to stay quietly where we are. They were, in short, the end of civilization as Ruskin knew it.[1]

Yet how quaint does Ruskin's cry of heartfelt protest now seem. Oddly enough, the railways of England were built accord-

1 See John Ruskin, *Railways in the Lake District* (1876), in *The Works of John Ruskin*, ed. E. T. Cook and Alexander Wedderburn, 39 vols, London, 1903–12, vol. 34, p. 141.

ing to designs influenced through and through by his writings, and in particular by *Stones of Venice*; they are looked back on now with intense nostalgia, as symbols of peace, place and distance. One of the most famous invocations of rural settlement in English – 'Adlestrop' by the poet Edward Thomas – describes a tranquil country railway station viewed from a train. And campaigners against automobiles propose the railways as their ideal of a safe, environmentally friendly and aesthetically pleasing link from place to place across a continent.

Ruskin's protest against the railways has lost its persuasive force. But it illustrates an important and recurring theme in the annals of human progress. For Ruskin, the railways threatened one of the fixed points in our moral universe, which is the earth itself – earth that provides the food we eat, the water we drink and the stones with which we build; earth that creates the distances between us, and also the comfort of settling side by side. When we build we must treat the land as a place of settlement, into which our lives are harmlessly slotted like those of fish in the sea. In a similar vein contemporary environmentalists complain that, by exploiting the earth for our ephemeral purposes, we treat as a mere means what should be respected as an end: we meddle with something that should be a fixed point for us, the place at which our self-centred experiments stop. Like Ruskin, the modern pessimist is urging us to consider what happens to *us* when old constraints are removed, old limitations abolished, and an old way of confronting the world replaced by an illusion of mastery.

In his novel *Erewhon*, published in 1872, Samuel Butler describes an imaginary country in which all machines are forbidden. The inhabitants had once availed themselves of watches, steam engines, mechanical pumps and hoists, and all the other devices that could be admired in the great Exhibitions of Victorian England. But, unlike Butler's Victorian contemporaries, they had perceived the terrible danger that these things represent. Machines, they realized, were always improving. Never for one moment did they take a step backwards into imperfections that they had surpassed.[2] Always the next machine was better, more versatile and more adapted to its uses than the last. Inevitably, therefore, the process of improvement would continue, until machines had no need of humans at all – until they were able to produce and reproduce themselves. At that point, like all creatures obedient to the law of evolution, the machines would be locked in a life-and-death struggle with their competitors. And their only competitor would be man. Hence, foreseeing that the machines would otherwise destroy them, the inhabitants of Erewhon had destroyed the machines.

The fear of the Erewhonians was not absurd: it had been anticipated by the machine-smashing Luddites of early nineteenth-century England, and was to return with twentieth-century agrarians like Hugh Massingham, Gustave Thibon and Wendell Berry. But its premise was unconvincing – at least to

---

2   Cf. Rilke, *Sonnets to Orpheus:* 'Alles Erworbene bedroht die Maschine... Nirgends bleibt sie zurück, daß wir ihr ein Mal entrönnen...'

Butler's readers. The idea of a self-reproducing machine seemed, to most of them, a mere literary fantasy. Yet sixty years later Aldous Huxley published *Brave New World*, the portrait of another imaginary country, in which humans are produced as machines are produced, according to specifications laid down by official policy. Intelligence, interests, pleasures and pains are all controlled, either genetically or by subsequent conditioning, and all those aspects of the human psyche in which eccentricities, commitments, deep emotions and old-fashioned virtues might take root, are deliberately prevented from forming. And if humans can be produced as machines are produced, in factories controlled by humans, why cannot machines be produced as humans are now produced, by self-reproduction?

Huxley's visionary future was a major advance on Butler's, since it engaged with what was actually happening in the surrounding world. Since 1931, when the book was published, advances in genetics, robotics and computer science have brought us face to face with the possibility that human beings might escape the limitations by which their lives have hitherto been circumscribed. The 'posthuman' future promises enhanced bodily and mental powers, immunity to disease and decay, even the conquest of death. And many argue that we have no choice but to embrace this condition: it will happen anyway, if only because biological science and medical technology are both moving in that direction. Why not learn to control the future, lest it should end, as in Huxley's dystopia, by controlling us? A new kind of optimist has therefore emerged, advocating a transformed human being who will emerge from the million years of man's incompetence to stuff the disasters back in Pandora's box.

In a celebrated play, *The Makropulos Case*, turned into an opera by Janáček, Karel Čapek explores the psyche of a woman who has inherited the elixir of eternal life and survived for 400 years, enjoying many times over the things at which human beings aim: pleasure, power, influence and love. And all these things have staled with repetition, her heart has hardened to every natural affection, and – being immortal – she looks on the frailty and need of her mortal lovers with an attitude of cold and cynical disgust. Her life is loveless, not because she cannot be offered love, but because she cannot receive it. All giving, all surrender, all sacrifice have vanished from her psyche, and only the empty lust for longevity remains. Suddenly realizing the depth of her unhappiness, she resolves to abandon the elixir and to let death have its prize. And in that moment she becomes human again, and lovable.

The moral made explicit in *The Makropulos Case* is implicit in art and literature down the centuries. Poetry, drama, portraiture and music show us that mortality is inextricably woven into the human scheme of things: that our virtues and our loves are the virtues and loves of dying creatures; that everything that leads us to cherish one another, to sacrifice ourselves, to make sublime and heroic gestures, is predicated on the assumption that we are vulnerable and transient, with only a fleeting claim on the things of this world. On such grounds Leon Kass, the American biologist and philosopher, has argued for what he calls the 'blessings of finitude' – for the intimate connection between the things that we value, and the fleetingness of life.[3]

All such reflections are dismissed by the advocates of the posthuman future. Ray Kurzweil, their most vocal spokesman, has predicted the emergence forty years hence of a 'singularity', a point at which technology will have advanced so far that human nature will be transcended.[4] The resulting 'transhuman' species will be the product of its own decisions, enjoying powers that no mere human has ever known. Kurzweil himself is an example, ebulliently advancing towards his future enhancement as the *Übermensch*, his computer-generated avatars sweeping before him into the furthest reaches of cyber-space. In one of Kurzweil's scenarios the world is saved from self-replicating nano-robots by a computer-screen avatar named Ramona. And Kurzweil registers neither alarm nor discontent at the thought of a world in which man's future has been bequeathed in this way to his own fictional creations. In that happy time people will be indistinguishable from the information contained in their brains, which could be immortalized in some benign central computer, to be downloaded into whatever cyborg might give it another go.

Huxley's anticipation of the effects of contraception and

---

3   Leon Kass, *Life, Liberty and the Defense of Dignity*, San Francisco, 2002.
4   Ray Kurzweil, *The Singularity is Near*, New York, 2005.

genetic engineering was amazingly prescient. But it did not prepare us for the transhumanists, for whom all the unsettling developments of recent technology are advances in science that only pig-headedness will prevent from being advances in freedom, happiness and power. Huxley and Čapek sought to show that the most important source of human value, and the thing that more than anything else justifies our being around for a while, is the capacity for love. Yet this capacity might be the first casualty of the transhuman world. For it will be a world in which human beings are without the need for those who love them while they are living and who grieve over them when they are dead.

While the worries of the pessimists remain the same, the advances that give rise to them change. Relationships, tranquillity, trust and love were jeopardized, Ruskin thought, by the railways; the same things were threatened, according to Butler, by the machines; Huxley wished to protect love and trust from sexual freedom and genetic engineering; Čapek saw the need to protect them from longevity, and therefore from medical progress; and the pessimists today see love and trust as the first casualties of the internet. Each spurt of optimism flies off in a new direction. And each time the call is made to respect the boundaries and the constraints without which love and trust will die.

Each time, moreover, the brave new worlds come nearer to the reality that inspires them. Kurzweil's, many think, is almost upon us, as the world-wide web threads its filaments into every human brain. In Kurzweil's future people morph into avatars, who peer at each other from the arctic vacancy of cyber-space. This is already happening, as we know from Facebook, MySpace and Second Life. By placing a screen between ourselves and others, while retaining control over what appears on it, we avoid the real encounter – forbidding to others the power and the freedom to challenge us in our deeper nature and to call on us here and now to take responsibility for ourselves and for them.

The sphere of freedom is one of responsibility, in which people pay for their freedoms by accounting for their use. The cyber-world therefore reminds us that freedom is as much threatened as it is enhanced by the new technologies. Although freedom is an exercise of the 'I', it comes into being through the 'we'; it cannot be assumed that people will still achieve freedom in a world where the 'we' is merely imagined and relationships and attachments no longer exist. Freedom in Huxley's dystopia was no more than the illusion of freedom; and with the loss of freedom came the loss of commitment and the loss of love. The transhumanists cheerfully promise a future like Huxley's, in which freedom, love and commitment disappear, but in which their loss can never be noticed by the new race of transhuman supernerds.

But freedom, love and commitment are essential to our projects. It is another dystopian work of fiction that made the point most powerfully, and long before Butler. When Mary Shelley envisaged the creation of Frankenstein's lonely monster, she saw that, if the monster was to be a human replica, it would have to be like us in other ways than its physical appearance and its animal life. It would have to be capable of hope and despair, admiration and contempt, love and hate. And in her story the monster became evil, as you or I might become evil, not because he was made that way, but because he searched the world for love and never found it. As we might put it, programmed into the monster were those moral capacities and emotional needs that are the core of human freedom. It is not that Frankenstein had to implant into the monster some peculiar spark of transcendence so as to endow it with free choice. With speech comes reason, with reason accountability, and with accountability all those emotions and states of mind that are the felt reality of freedom.

In the conflict between the optimists and the dystopians we therefore encounter a deeper dispute concerning the place of the future in our thinking. As a rational agent I see the world as a theatre of action in which I and my goals take a central place. I act to increase my power, to acquire the means to realize my objectives, to bring others to my side and to work with them to overcome the obstacles that thwart me. This 'I' attitude is implanted deep in the psyche. The 'I' reaches out to the future and asserts its prerogative. It is infinite in ambition and recognizes no limits, but only obstacles. In emergencies the 'I' takes command, and seizes whatever can enhance its power or amplify its scope. Whatever human ingenuity can discover it will happily put to its use, weighing the cost and the benefit, but regarding nothing as immovably fixed, and no obstacle as anything more than an obstacle. The optimist will therefore venture boldly into cyber-space, as into the world of genetic engineering, seeing opportunities to enhance the power and scope of the individual, and careless of the constants that, in the end, we depend upon, if anything at all is to make sense to us. Thus it is that Mustapha Mond, in Huxley's fiction, praises the world that he controls – one in which all obstacles to happiness, human nature included, have been removed, and in which all desires are satisfied, since the desire and the thing desired are manufactured together. And yet this world is one that does not contain us, and from which we turn away in apprehension. And the same is true of the cyber-world of Kurzweil, a world consciously created as an illusion, purchased at the cost of the only things we really value.

Behind all our projects, like a horizon against which they are projected, is another and quite different attitude. I am aware that I belong to a kind, and that kind has a place in nature. I am also aware that I depend upon others in countless ways that make it imperative to seek their approval. Whereas the 'I' attitude seeks change and improvement, overcoming the challenges presented by nature, the 'we' attitude seeks stasis and accommodation, in which we are at one with each other and with the world. Things that threaten our need for adaptation, by entirely destroying our environment, by undermining human nature, or by eroding the conditions under which free cooperation is possible, awaken in us a profound sense of unease, even of sacrilege. The 'we' attitude recognizes limits and constraints, boundaries that we cannot transgress and that create the frame that gives meaning to our hopes. Moreover, it stands back from the goals of the 'I', is prepared to renounce its purposes, however precious, for the sake of the long-term benefits of love and friendship. It takes a negotiating posture towards the other, and seeks to share not goals but constraints. It is finite in ambition and easily deflected; and it is prepared to trade increases in power and scope for the more rewarding goods of social affection.

The optimist will protest that human nature does not stand still. Even without genetic engineering and virtual reality, the 'I' attitude restlessly pursues the path of invention, and in so doing radically changes the focus and the goal of human conduct. Human nature is plastic, and it did not need biotechnology or the internet to persuade us of this: it is surely implausible to say that the human being of today, raised in a condition of material abundance, cushioned against disasters that to our ancestors were part of the normal cost of being alive, is the same kind of being as the one who painted the murals in the Lascaux caves. On the contrary, the new human being is on the way to controlling the forces by which his ancestors were controlled: disease, aggression, even the threat of death itself. He might even obtain a kind of immortality, as Kurzweil suggests, by storing the information-content of his brain on a computer, from which it can be downloaded into future cyborgs.

By contrast, tales like those of Mary Shelley, Huxley and Čapek remind us that our moral concepts are rooted in the 'we' attitude that is threatened by the careless pursuit of mastery.

When we envisage situations that involve a reshaping of human nature, so that all those features that traditional morality was designed to regulate – aggression, fragility, mortality; love, hope, desire – either disappear or are purged of their costs, then we conjure worlds that we cannot understand and that do not in fact contain us. What looks to the optimist like a gain in freedom is seen by the pessimist as a loss of it. Were we, like Huxley's savage, to find ourselves washed up on those imagined shores, we should be as unconsoled as he, finding ourselves not among fellow people but among machines.

The dispute between the unscrupulous optimists and the dystopians will not disappear, but will be endlessly renewed as new futures occur to the one, and a renewed past detains the other. In all emergencies, and all changes that abolish old routines, the optimists hope to turn things to their benefit. They are as likely to consult the past as a battalion fighting for its life in a city is likely to protect the monuments. They strive to be on the winning side, and to find the path into the future on which the light of 'I' stays shining.

The 'we' attitude, by contrast, is circumspect. It sees human decisions as *situated*, constrained by place, time and community; by custom, faith and law. It urges us not to throw ourselves always into the swim of things, but to stand aside and reflect. It emphasizes *constraints* and *boundaries*, and reminds us of human imperfection and of the fragility of real communities. Its decisions take account of other people and other times. In its deliberations the dead and the unborn have an equal voice with the living. And its attitude to those who say 'press on' and 'ever onward' is 'sufficient unto the day is the evil thereof'. It does not endorse a comprehensive pessimism, but only the occasional *dose* of pessimism, with which to temper hopes that otherwise might ruin us. It is the voice of wisdom in a world of noise. And for that very reason, no one hears it.

TWO

The Best Case Fallacy

Let him in whose ears the low-voiced Best is killed by the clash of the First,
Who holds that if way to the Better there be, it exacts a full look at the
Worst,
Who feels that delight is a delicate growth cramped by crookedness, custom,
and fear,
Get him up and be gone as one shaped awry; he disturbs the order here.

'In Tenebris' by Thomas Hardy

The poet and historian Robert Conquest once announced three 'laws of politics', the first of which states that everyone is right-wing about what he knows best.[5] By 'right-wing' Conquest meant suspicious of enthusiasm and novelty, and respectful towards hierarchy, tradition and established ways. One sign of ignorance, according to Conquest, is the preference for originality over

---

5   The other two laws are: (2) any organization not explicitly right-wing sooner or later becomes left-wing, and (3) the simplest way to explain the behaviour of any bureacratic organization is to assume that it is controlled by a cabal of its enemies.

custom and radical solutions over traditional authority. Of course, we need originality, just as we may need radical solutions, when circumstances radically change. But we need these things when conditions are exceptional, and it is against the desire to see all cases as exceptional that Conquest was warning.

Conquest was writing as a conservative in an academic climate dominated by the political left. His own career had been blighted by advancing pessimistic arguments about communism, at a time when optimists had hit on communism as the proof of their hopes.[6] But what Conquest meant is of wider significance. When it comes to our own lives, to the things that we know and in which we have acquired both understanding and competence, we take a measured view. To call this measured view 'right-wing' or 'conservative' is, of course, to make an assumption about politics that many would reject. But the point remains. The midwife who knows her job respects the solutions that have been proved by the generations who preceded her; she recognizes those with authority and instinctively obeys their advice. And she does not hesitate to offer advice of her own. She measures her own judgement against the accumulated wisdom of tradition, and if she takes a risk, because the problem before her is without a clear precedent, she is careful to measure the cost of failure and to ensure that it can be borne.

6   Conquest's *magnum opus*, *The Great Terror*, was published in 1968 to considerable acclaim. For many it was a triumphant vindication of his anti-communist stance; for others it was merely further proof that he was not fit to teach in a university.

Such a person is not a pessimist; she is what might be called a scrupulous optimist – one who measures the extent of a problem and consults the existing store of knowledge and authority in order to solve it, relying on initiative and inspiration when no other guidance can be found, or when some original quirk in her predicament sparks off a matching response in herself. In all that we know most about, and in every relationship that is dear to us, our attitude is, or is normally, scrupulous in just that way. We have acquired what competence we can and know where to look for advice and guidance. And when we encounter weaknesses or make mistakes, we strive to better ourselves. We are acutely aware that we are only one among many in our field of expertise, are ready to defer to those with knowledge and experience, and are more respectful of the accumulated store of others' knowledge than the scant addition we might make to it ourselves. It is with an educated sense of the first-person plural that we deploy the knowledge that is our securest personal possession.

This scrupulous optimism also knows the uses of pessimism, and when to qualify our plans with a dose of it. It encourages us to count the cost of failure, to form a conception of the worst case, and to take risks in full consciousness of what will happen if the risks don't pay. Unscrupulous optimism is not like that. It makes leaps of thought that are not leaps of faith but refusals to acknowledge that reason has withdrawn its support from them. It does not count the cost of failure or imagine the worst case scenario. On the contrary, it is typified by what I shall call the 'best case' fallacy. Asked to choose under conditions of uncertainty, it imagines the best outcome and assumes that it need consider no other. It devotes itself to the one result, and either forgets to count the cost of failure, or else – and this is its most pernicious aspect – contrives to bequeath that cost to someone else.

The best case fallacy is the mindset of the gambler. It is sometimes said that gamblers are risk-takers and that this, at least, can be admired in them, that they have the courage to risk what they have in the game that attracts them. That is, in fact, the opposite of the truth. Gamblers are not risk-takers at all; they enter the game in full expectation of winning it, led by their illusions to bask in an unreal sense of safety. In their own eyes they are not taking a risk, but simply proceeding towards a predetermined goal with the full cooperation of their faculties and their God-given luck. They have estimated the best case, in which their fortune has been secured by their master-throw of the dice, and that is the outcome towards which they are inexorably tending. The worst case, in which they and their family are ruined, occurs to them if at all only as something for which they cannot be blamed – a stroke of fate that is bound to be compensated by some future success, and in itself a source of pleasure in making that success the more inevitable. This is the character described by Dostoevsky in *The Gambler* – his own character, which brought devastation on himself and his family. And it is the character of the unscrupulous optimist in every sphere.

We have a more telling instance in the current 'credit crunch'.

Many factors conspired to produce this crisis. But we do not need to look far to discover the best case fallacy at the heart of it. The first stirrings can be perceived in the Community Reinvestment Act, signed into law by America's President Carter in 1977. This requires banks and other lenders to offer mortgages in a way that addresses 'the credit needs of the communities' in which they work, and in particular the needs of low-income and minority households. In short, it requires them to set aside the normal reasoning of lenders concerning the security of a debt, and to offer credit as a part of social policy and not as a business deal. The reasoning behind the act was an impeccable piece of optimism, beginning from the best case scenario, according to which otherwise disadvantaged groups would be lifted into the realm of home-ownership, so taking their first step towards the American dream. Everyone would benefit from this, and no one more than the banks who had helped their communities to flourish. In the event, of course, the banks who had been pressured into ignoring the old demands of prudence, and who had been forbidden by law to consult the worst case scenario, ended with a steadily growing accumulation of bad debts, leading eventually to the 'subprime mortgage crisis' of 2008.

Others, meanwhile, had begun to trade in these debts. After all, the best case scenario tells us that a mortgage, being secured on a home and therefore on the one thing in which every borrower has the greatest investment, cannot fail to pay interest. And a fixed rate mortgage can be sold at a profit, when interest rates fall below the rate agreed. The worst case scenario – so obvious that nobody bothered to check it out – tells us that, when interest rates fall, money loses its value, and fixed rates become harder to pay. The good debt becomes bad, however much was invested in the home that secures it.

Some will argue that the fault here lies not in the optimism, but in the unrealistic view of human nature that underlies it. It seems to me, however, that the fault lies deeper. There is a kind of *addiction* to unreality that informs the most destructive forms of optimism: a desire to cross out reality, as the premise from which practical reason begins, and to replace it with a system of compliant illusions. 'Futurism' is like this. The excited description of future possibilities that you find in the writings of Buckminster Fuller[7] and Ray Kurzweil, and in the fantasies of the transhumanists and the cybernerds, owes its appeal to the unrealities that it brings before the reader's mind. In these writings we see the deep appeal of the future tense. By changing 'is' to 'will be' we enable the unreal to trump the actual, and worlds without limits to obliterate the constraints that we know.

The same addiction to unreality can be seen in the attitude to credit. A small dose of pessimism would remind us that, when people fund current consumption by borrowing against the

---

7   All but forgotten now, this transhumanist *avant la lettre* was the darling of progressive architects, social reformers and Panglossians in the sixties. See 'Buckminster Fuller', in Roger Scruton, *The Politics of Culture and Other Essays*, Manchester, 1981.

future, they are dealing with an unreal asset — the promise of future production — and that a thousand contingencies might arise to prevent that asset from being realized. A credit economy therefore depends upon a shared trust in human nature and in the power of promises, in circumstances where the obligation to keep promises is less and less acknowledged, precisely because people are acquiring the habit of postponing their debts. In these circumstances a peculiar illusion takes over. People cease to see the financial world as composed of human beings, with all their moral weaknesses and self-interested schemes, and see it instead as composed of graphs and indices — figures that in turn represent shares, interest rates, currencies, things that can be traded for human energy but which in themselves are mere abstractions, whose economic value depends solely on people's trust in them. The stock market takes on, in their thinking, the character of a great animated cartoon, in which things move on the screen as though propelled by a life of their own, even though the screen itself is merely a distant projection of the actions and desires of people. The fundamental moral truth, which a small dose of pessimism would have made central to all the decisions on which the market depends, is that credit depends on trust, that trust depends upon responsibility and that, in a credit economy, in which people seek to enjoy now and pay later, responsibility is constantly dwindling, leaking from the system through the very mechanism that depends on it.

Of course, if the cost of defaulting falls squarely on the

culprit, and the interests of the creditor are secured by a strong law of bankruptcy, there is no reason for trust to leak from the system. But laws of bankruptcy have been weakened and credit made easy, precisely so as to enjoy the short-term benefits of an economy in which the best case fallacy prevails. That such an economy cannot last is obvious; but while it lasts it rejoices in the fictions that propel it.

'Money illusions', whereby graphs and numbers exert their spell over people whose energies they represent, can be witnessed down the centuries. Like the gambler, the speculator sees reality in superstitious terms, animated by forces that are tending of their own accord towards profit, bringing pleasure and abundance here and now, and never confronting the clever player with the cost of them. It has been one of the historic roles of the prophet to warn against this kind of self-perpetuating illusion, to bring people face to face with the unreality of their hopes, when those hopes have been transcribed onto the screen of monetary fortune. Muhammad was such a prophet, and his objection to taking interest repeats an ancient hostility to money and its charms. It was not borrowing and lending that Muhammad objected to, nor the mechanism of debt – for these are ways in which moral beings can benefit each other, by relying on a shared fund of virtue. What Muhammad objected to was the growth of what one might call 'unreal estate'. It seemed to him that you don't make a contribution to the economy merely by *owning* things. We flourish as a community because goods are produced and distributed among us, and because each person is able to satisfy his needs by contributing his labour.

Moreover, suppose we allow people to earn interest on loans: does there not arise a strange spectral economy, in which people trade in debts – John lending to Bill, and then selling Bill's debt to Henry at a profit? What kind of trade is this, in which the subject matter is simply a negative cipher in a bank statement? Furthermore, John can insure his debt against Bill's failure to pay, so that, whatever happens, he will make a return on his capital, having used it for no other purpose than to create a rent on Bill's labour. To the Prophet this seemed like the Devil's work: to make the whole productive process dependent upon the trade in unreal goods, and furthermore to pre-empt the will of God by insuring against failure. Contracts of insurance were thus forbidden by the original Islamic jurists, along with any loan that involved a rent on another's production, rather than an offer of deferred payment for a service.

Islamic law has gone further, refusing to recognize either the rights or the duties of corporations, which are – from the moral point of view – mere fictions. It has therefore never accepted the idea of a 'limited liability company', which again seems like a device for evading responsibility. After all, it is limited liability that has enabled company directors to ruin their employees and shareholders while rewarding themselves with massive bonuses. In a sense there is no more vivid example of 'unreal estate': for the devoted adherent of Islam what we are witnessing, with the collapse of Wall Street, is the sudden disappearance of a dream.

Muhammad's economic reasoning was flawed. Interest is the compensation for the risk of lending, and therefore the proper price of money. The limited liability company is not, or should not be, a device for shielding the directors from liability, but a device for making them answerable to shareholders. It is also a very effective device, being responsible for the rise of the great trading economies in seventeenth-century Holland and England. All the things against which the Prophet complained have a proper use, insurance included. Nevertheless, he was right in thinking that they also have a misuse – a misuse in which speculators put the *worst case* out of mind. And they put it out of mind because of their addiction to unrealities – and in particular to the illusions which suggest that you can always transfer the cost of failure.

Prophets are *systematic* pessimists: they take the imperfections of the human world as defining it, and offer to replace it with another kind of unreal hope – in the case of Muhammad, the hope of a childishly conceived Heaven, which is even more fully supplied with illusions than the world below. In recommending the uses of pessimism I do not wish to endorse such nonsense, or to argue for the kind of systematic pessimism that informs many of the prophets of the Old Testament, full of wisdom though their writings are. Nevertheless, it is worth reflecting on Muhammad's counsels. For they are the counsels of someone who – precisely because he had invested his illusions in another world – perceived the reality of this world so much the more clearly. He would have warned against the insane proliferation of risks that comes about when people are not personally liable for failure and think that they can insure against risk in any case – putting out of mind the obvious fact that insurance companies can collapse like any other, and are the more likely to collapse the more risks we transfer to them. And maybe he would have gone on to point out that it is this habit of pre-empting God's will – of thinking that we can always transfer the cost of our risk-taking – that has led to the crazy notion that, when all else fails, the government will step in to save us. Don't governments fail? And are they not more likely to fail, the more they borrow from the taxpayer? It surely matters little that their borrowing is coercive, and that they can shift things around for a while in order to cover up the hole in their accounts. In the end this escalating trade in unreal estate will come to a halt, and everybody will look down at what he has been holding in his hands and furiously trading with his neighbours, to discover that it is just a piece of paper on which there is nothing written save an empty promise.

There is no greater contrast of character than that between Muhammad and John Maynard Keynes, the flippant aesthete, lover of Lytton Strachey and Duncan Grant, and leading light of the Cambridge Apostles, who was also the greatest influence on economic policies during the first half of the twentieth century. Muhammad warned against interest and insurance because each involves transferring a debt to the future, which belongs not to men but to God. Keynes took the opposite view, famously declaring that 'in the long run we are all dead' – in other words, the more we can postpone to the future, the less we will have to account for it. In the face of an economic downturn, governments should stimulate demand, embarking on large-scale projects that will bring employment to the millions, who will spend their money here and now, so creating more demand, which will in turn create more jobs, which will…

Is this just another example of one of those 'money illusions' against which the prophets warn? Is this just building one promise on another in an infinite regress of transferred liability, so that no one is really committed? A dose of natural pessimism would suggest as much. But Keynes did not see things that way. Governments can stimulate demand by borrowing money against their own credibility, and nothing is more credible than a government. And when the time for payment comes, the government can borrow more, so constantly shifting its obligations to future generations who, after all, are not part of any long run in which *we* will exist. And the strange thing is that a government stealing from the next generation in order to buy the votes of the present one is supposed to be perfectly acceptable, while Bernard Madoff is now facing many years in jail, accused of doing the same. The contrast with Muhammad's religious view, based as it is on the eternal liability of all of us here and now, could not be more telling. To be fair, Keynes intended his recommendations for emergencies only, and warned against the debasing of the currency that would ensue if they were built into the structure of government. But the emphasis placed, in *The General Theory of Employment, Interest and Money*, on the role of government in stimulating demand has carried the day.[8] The American government is now borrowing trillions of dollars from future taxpayers in order to maintain the present trade in luxuries, all purchased on credit by people who don't regard credit as a debt to be paid, but merely as a march stolen on the fool who offers it. And governments around the world are following suit.

There are those who argue that the adoption of Keynes's strategy at the time of the New Deal caused the Depression to deepen, and postponed by twenty years the recovery of Western economies, meanwhile making war in Europe inevitable, as Germany chose the quick route out of recession.[9] I don't know whether this is true. Indeed, I don't know whether anything that economists say is true. For almost all of them argue as though it

---

8   Academic economists later argued that credit stimulates demand and is the prime mover of economic production, a view that invites the kind of government intervention that is associated with Keynes. See especially the two interventions by Ben S. Bernanke, appointed chairman of the Federal Reserve in 2006: Ben S. Bernanke and Alan S. Blinder, 'Credit, Money and Aggregate Demand', *American Economic Review*, vol. 78, no. 2, May 1988; and Ben S. Bernanke and Mark Gertler, 'Inside the Black Box: the Credit Channel of Monetary Policy Transmission', NBER Working Papers 5146, 1995.

9   See Amity Shlaes, *The Forgotten Man: a New History of the Great Depression*, New York, 2007.

were not human beings who are the subject of their discipline, but 'profit maximizers', people wholly immersed in and dominated by the 'I' attitude, acting according to the principles of cost and benefit, and never troubling to make the distinction between real and unreal products, between right and wrong ways of behaving, and between responsible and irresponsible attitudes to present and future others. A dose of pessimism ought surely to warn us against such a science. Its results are seldom the subject of agreement among those who study them, and its recommendations seem to depend more on the political assumptions of their proponents than on any agreed method of enquiry.

Having said as much, I should add that I regard the systematic pessimism of prophets like Jeremiah as no less replete with illusions, and no less destructive of ordinary reasonableness, than the unscrupulous optimism against which it is directed. I do not see the credit crisis as a refutation of free market principles, as a 'crisis of capitalism' or as the downfall of the global economy. I see it simply as showing how things get out of hand as soon as fallacious ways of reasoning become locked into policies. The free market, and the risk-taking that is generic to enterprise, are human goods, exemplary manifestations of our collective rationality and, provided they are tempered by a dose of pessimism, far superior to the known alternatives. Set within the constraints that define the 'we', the market provides the only peaceful solution to the problem of coordination in a society of strangers. This, however, is a topic to which I return in considering the 'planning fallacy' and the 'zero sum fallacy'. More useful at this juncture is a portrait of the scrupulous optimist, and the uses to which his pessimistic leanings are put.

Scrupulous optimists know that they live in a world of constraints, that altering these constraints is difficult and that the consequences of doing so are often unpredictable. They know that they can far more easily adjust *themselves* than the constraints under which they live, and that they should work on this continuously, not only for the sake of their own happiness and of those they love and who depend on them, but also for the sake of the 'we' attitude that respects the constants on which our values depend, and which does its best to preserve them.

Like all rational beings, scrupulous optimists are risk-takers. This does not mean that they are gamblers, who deceive themselves with fictions of their own inexorable good luck. On the contrary. They take risks as part of their desire to improve things, always counting the cost of failure and evaluating the worst case scenario. They recognize that risks are both the school of practical reasoning and the opportunity to improve things. Their guiding principles are two: that they are free to act, and that they themselves are responsible for the outcome. Hence they assess each situation as it arises, make realistic assumptions about others, and strive to honour their commitments and to settle their debts.

In the crisis through which we are living now, such people will not necessarily have done better than their less scrupulous or more prophetically inclined contemporaries. Like others, they would have been tempted by the stock-market bubble; they would have been tempted by the banks and money-lenders, with their promises of endless credit and their determination to hide the long-term cost of it. They would have recognized, in the global economy, opportunities for risk-taking that could be justified on the information available. On the other hand, they would have known one thing that the world was striving to put out of mind, which is that when people are being everywhere tempted into debt, there will be a growing and eventually worldwide reluctance to pay up, that honesty will be increasingly seen as a weakness, and that eventually the habit will arise of paying off one debt by contracting another. At a certain moment the foundation of trust will be withdrawn and the structure built on it will crumble to dust.

Most important of all, scrupulous optimists strive to fix their hopes as best they can on the things they know and understand, on the people who are close to them, and on the small-scale local affections that are the foundation of our happiness. They know that they are vulnerable, like everyone, to external and public events, and that they must take provision against them. They know that they are members of a community, a nation and a species, all of which must take collective action for their survival. But their pessimism tells them that the lot of communities is not improved by unfounded hope, that small-scale work is the best route to peace and conciliation, and that rootless hopes are as much a threat to the human future as the dangers they hide from us. It also tells them that freedom means responsibility, and that a society in which people strive constantly to transfer the costs of failure is a society of 'I's without a 'we'.

Paradoxical though this may seem, therefore, such people are more likely to exhibit public spirit, local patriotism and the core impulses of *agape* or neighbour-love than those who entertain themselves with exultant hopes for the human future. Optimists who have transferred their hope with whatever triumphant fanfares to the sphere of necessary things have also relieved themselves of the need to take personal action. Their thought is that of Shelley's apophthegm: 'Man, oh, not men!', to which they will add that the plans, schemes and reforms that they have devised will abolish the old constraints and imperfections without their help, and in any case they are far too busy. After all, it is precisely in order to free themselves from worries that optimists think as they do. They have abolished the 'we' feeling, with its apprehensions and trepidations, and invested the world with a universal 'I' – an 'I' that is in some way looking after things. There is no need to volunteer at the hospital or the youth club, to join the rescue service or to organize a fête, when all such problems have been solved by a central plan. If optimists get involved nevertheless, it is seldom in order to give their time and energy to people they know or to local causes they understand, but to campaign for some large-scale alteration in the scheme of things – some redeeming transformation, the consequences of which are as unknowable to them as they are to everyone else.

Judicious pessimism teaches us not to idolize human beings, but to forgive their faults and to strive in private for their amendment. It teaches us to limit our ambitions in the public sphere, and to keep open the institutions, customs and procedures whereby mistakes are corrected and faults confessed to, rather than to aim for some new arrangement in which mistakes are never made. The worst kind of optimism is that which animated Lenin and the Bolsheviks, which caused them to believe that they had set mankind on a path to the solution of history's residual problems, and which caused them also to destroy all the institutions and procedures through which mistakes can be corrected. The resulting machine without feedback carried on functioning, it is true, for another seventy years. But by the time it crashed, sixty million people had died as a result of the folly and wickedness that had been programmed into it, and the society that survived the crash was (and is) arguably the most demoralized that the world has ever known.

The issue of revolutionary optimism will occupy me at several points in the chapters that follow. But it is worth pausing now to recognize one consequence of the fallacies that I shall be exploring, which exist in order to project hope outwards, onto the public world. Whole lifestyles are built upon these fallacies, and they confer upon those who espouse them a validation and a cost-free serenity that could never be achieved were they to invest their hopes in themselves and in the things upon which they can act with proper understanding. When these fallacies are questioned, therefore, optimists are apt to release a flood of defensive anger.

Rather than examine their beliefs and risk the great cost of correcting them, they will turn upon their critics and issue quasi-religious anathemas, of the kind that issued from the pens of the French and Russian Revolutionaries and which have had such a toxic effect on public debate in modern times. The critics of unscrupulous optimists are not just mistaken in their eyes, but evil, concerned to destroy the hopes of all mankind, and to replace genial kindness towards our species with a cruel cynicism. We should not be surprised, therefore, when we look back over the great conflicts that have torn the world apart since the Enlightenment, to discover that optimists have been far ahead of pessimists in their expressions of anger, and that the great crimes – the Holocaust and the Gulag included – should be laid, in the end, at the doors of those who were drunk on false hopes. In what follows I give some examples that illustrate what I have in mind, but I know that no optimist will be persuaded by them. It is one of the most remarkable features of the optimistic mindset that it will never accept responsibility for the effects of its own beliefs, or acknowledge the danger of the fallacies that have guided it. There is simply *no way* in which the fallacies that I examine in this book can ever release the mind that has fallen into them. This is a mystery, but I hope in the course of my argument to cast some light on it. The least that can be said is that the fallacies that concern me are not mistakes that stand to be corrected, but doors that shut behind those who enter them, and retain them forever in darkness.

But is it not part of human nature to hope in this way, and to hope beyond the limitations of a private life and the small-scale promptings of a narrow and localized public spirit? Have not religions always been fed from this hope, and is this not the message of St Paul, that faith, hope and love stand and fall together, so that to act as we should towards our neighbours, we must also live in hope for them? It is true that religions in the Abrahamic tradition offer hope: they promise a safe conduct from the prison of this world into the life everlasting, and the arduousness of the life they command here below is compensated by an infinite reward hereafter. But the effect of optimism on this scale is not dissimilar from the effect of moderate pessimism. The message as understood by the ordinary believer is that the kingdom of God is not of this world, that we should proceed in this life with the caution that our instincts suggest to us, and that any attempt to build Heaven on earth will be both presumptuous and irrational. We are stewards of the earth and of our own frail nature, and by despatching our hopes to that celestial sphere where they do no damage, we are able to adopt the 'we' attitude that is the only known safeguard of our collective assets here below.

Indeed, it is arguably one of the functions of religion that it neutralizes optimism. By transferring our more speculative hopes from the arena of worldly action to a sphere that we cannot alter, a transcendental faith frees us from the need to believe that radical changes are within our power. It offers an opening to pessimism, and one that we witness also in primitive religions, with their emphasis on piety and caution in worldly affairs, and on the danger of pre-empting the will of the gods. 'Piety,' as Santayana puts it, 'is the spirit's acknowledgement of its incarnation.'[10] It is 'more closely linked with custom than with thought', and the one who lacks it altogether is rootless, wandering 'from place to place, a voluntary exile, always querulous, always uneasy, always alone'. I hope that, by the end of this book, the reader will recognize the truth in Santayana's remarks.

Unscrupulous optimists, whose goal-directed worldview recognizes only obstacles but never constraints, are alone in the world. Their cheerfulness is only skin-deep, a mask that hides a profound disquiet, lest the plank of illusions cease to support them. The principal use of pessimism is to retreat from that lonely posture into the true first-person plural. Scrupulous people, who temper hope with a dose of pessimism, are those who recognize constraints, not obstacles. There are things they will not consider and things they cannot do, since these things threaten the framework required by individual responsibility and by the consensual norms of the community. The 'we' attitude looks on our plans and schemes from a point of view outside them, often taking an ironical attitude to human aspirations, and regarding the most important social outcomes as unpredictable by-products of our agreements, rather than shared collective goals.

It is this last feature that is perhaps the most distinctive contri-

10 George Santayana, *The Life of Reason*, London, 1905, p. 184.

bution of the 'we' response, and it is one that will occupy me at several points in the chapters that follow. Scrupulous people see the order of society not as something imposed as a goal and achieved by shared effort, but as something emerging by an 'invisible hand' from decisions and agreements that did not intend it. They accept the world and its imperfections, not because it cannot be improved, but because many of the improvements that matter are by-products of our cooperation rather than the goal of it. They recognize that the invisible hand produces bad results as well as good, and that there is a need for leadership and guidance if emergencies are to be successfully managed. But they also acknowledge that wisdom is seldom contained in a single head, and is more likely to be enshrined in customs that have stood the test of time than in the schemes of radicals and activists. Such people get a bad press, of course. But that is because the press is dominated by radicals and activists.

THREE

The Born Free Fallacy

Rousseau's *Social Contract* famously announces that man is born free, but is everywhere in chains. Whether Rousseau was an optimist is a matter of dispute among scholars; whether he believed what he wrote will be forever uncertain; and whether his claim of honesty in *The Confessions* is a case of protesting too much will also never be finally decided. *The Social Contract* ends by justifying the chains that it begins by lamenting, and its passionate defence of liberty was later used to excuse the tyranny of the Revolutionaries. But one thing is clear: Rousseau provided the language, and the avenues of thought, with which to introduce a new conception of human freedom, according to which freedom is what is left when we take all institutions, all restraints, all laws and all hierarchies away. And his followers believed that this freedom, once obtained, would express itself in the happiness and brotherhood of mankind, and not in that 'war of all against all' that Hobbes had described as the true 'state of nature'. It was

Rousseau's way of thinking that led to the following utterance of Mirabeau, who died before seeing it refuted: 'General liberty will rid the world of the absurd oppressions that overwhelm humanity. It will give rise to a rebirth of that universal brotherhood without which all public and private benefit is so uncertain and precarious.' A short while later Robespierre was establishing what he called 'the despotism of liberty', cutting off any head that had a problem with it. The final death toll, according to the French historian René Sédillot, was two million, with Europe meanwhile embroiled in the continent-wide wars that were to destroy the hopes of more reasonable people.[11]

Now I don't wish to suggest that the French Revolution was caused by a fallacious idea. That would be to simplify this great event beyond caricature.[12] But the acquiescence of the Revolutionaries in the havoc that they caused was certainly made easier by the effortless optimism of their philosophy. And that philosophy suffered not the slightest setback from its visible disproof, so exemplifying the extraordinary feature of unscrupulous optimists that I noted in the last chapter – their ability to believe the impossible in the face of all adverse evidence. The very same idea of freedom, as the natural condition of mankind, which wants only the elimination of institutions, structures and

11 René Sédillot, *Le coût de la Révolution française*, Paris, 1986.

12 I have given an account of the French revolutionary psyche, however, in 'Man's Second Disobedience', in *The Philosopher on Dover Beach*, Manchester and South Bend, IN, 1999.

hierarchies to realize, has endured in politics, in education and in the philosophy of art, right down to the present day. It underpinned the sexual revolution, the 'relevance revolution' in education and the social upheavals of 1968. In this chapter I consider one or two of those examples, in order to identify the places where a small dose of pessimism might have rectified a large and damaging mistake.

But first, it is necessary to identify the fallacy; to clarify just why it is that human beings are *not* born free. Institutions, laws, restraints and moral discipline are a *part* of freedom and not its enemy, and liberation from such things rapidly brings freedom to an end. The point has been made in many ways and in many tones of voice down the ages, but perhaps never more persuasively than by Hegel, whose complex arguments might be put in the following simplified form.[13]

Let us imagine a world in which people find themselves in a state of nature, without laws or social norms, each fending for himself in competition for life's resources. It is tempting to see this as a condition of perfect freedom: after all, there are no constraints of a social kind, no laws or customs, and what individuals want is the only authority governing what they should do to claim it. However, the state of nature contains others, equally intent on pursuing their own desires, and in competition for the

13 I refer to *The Phenomenology of Spirit*, Chapter 4, Part 1, and draw to some extent on Alexandre Kojève, ed. R. Queneau, *Introduction à la lecture de Hegel*, Paris, 1947.

world's resources. The existence of others is the primary constraint on action, and the absence of laws in no way liberates me from that constraint but on the contrary places it firmly in the way of everything I do. Inevitably what I want, in that state of nature, will be wanted also by my rivals – for nothing determines our desires besides our shared human nature. I will be in competition with the other for the thing that I desire and, in conditions of scarcity in which one of us alone can actually possess it, this competition will take the form of war. There will be a 'life-and-death struggle', as Hegel puts it, for the resources that both of us need.

Such a struggle is resolved in one of two ways: either one party kills the other, or one of them gives up. In the first case there is no change to the basic situation. The victor is triumphant in getting what he wants and awaits the next mortal conflict to test his powers. In the second case, however, the basic situation changes. One party has shown that he prefers life to freedom, and that he is prepared to surrender his will in the face of conflict. In other words, he adopts the position of a subordinate, and implicitly confers on the other the status of master. The conflict between them, instead of resolving itself in death, resolves itself in a new kind of human relationship – that of domination. A primeval residue of this relationship exists in all of us, like the genetic trace of an old and long-surpassed adaptation. And we witness this in infants, who scream for what they want, enter into conflict with others who want the same, and resolve their conflicts, if no adult intervenes, in relations of power, with one party bullying and the other giving way.

Hegel describes the relation of master and slave as one in which freedom has been lost – but lost by both parties, because neither really possessed it. The 'freedom' available in a state of nature is an illusion – a mere lack of constraint, but without the security and the recognition that endow freedom with its distinctively human attributes. It is the freedom of the untamed 'I', who can roam as he wills, but who has no conception of the value of being here rather than there, of gaining one thing rather than another, since he has no sense of the 'we' who would endorse his objectives. He, the supposed master, is a self without self-knowledge, a self in its 'immediacy', who desires things but has no sense of their value. True freedom involves not just doing what you want, but valuing what you get. It involves planning, intending, having reasons for action and achieving what you set out to accomplish. And Hegel's ruling thought is that all these features are essentially *social* features of the will: they depend upon the human relations in which our actions and emotions are embedded, and are not available outside the context provided by the rules and customs of a language-using community, and the mutually recognized constraints through which we do not merely pursue our desires but also renounce them.

Hegel illustrates this through a critical examination of the master–slave relationship. Suppose one party has control of another, so as to be released from the need to expend his own energy in the satisfaction of his wants. What conception will he acquire of the value of the things that he receives? That I want something is no guarantee of its value: not unless I also have a sense of my *own* value, as a being whose right to exist is duly acknowledged, and whose desires and needs are recognized as legitimate. The master can demand this kind of acknowledgement from his slave, but can he know that he receives it? To command acknowledgement and respect is easy, if one has achieved a position of command. But respect that is commanded is not real respect: only if freely given does respect amount to an acknowledgement of one's right to it. And the slave is not in a position freely to give what his master demands of him.

The slave likewise receives no respect from his master, who takes a purely instrumental attitude to this being under his yoke. However, the slave has another route to respect, which is the route of labour. He acts on the world, and imprints his will on the product. He acquires, through his activity, an enhanced consciousness of the worth of what he does. He sees the result of his labour as *my* work. He makes the world in his own image, even if not for his own use. His self-consciousness grows, and although the master treats him as a means, he has a growing sense of his own value – not as a means but as an end. His outer enslavement masks an inner freedom that grows with the exercise of his creative powers.

Hegel's original thought was that the inner freedom of the slave matches an inner lassitude in the master, and that in due course the tension within their relationship causes the slave to assert the powers and the self-knowledge that he has acquired through labour, to reduce the pampered master to servitude, and so to reverse their status – a dialectical process illustrated by Strindberg in *Miss Julie*, and by Robin Maugham in his novel *The Servant*, made into a well-known film by Harold Pinter and Joseph Losey. This reversal of the conflict serves to perpetuate it. Hence the master–slave relationship subjugates both parties to the rule of self-interest, and deprives both of genuine freedom.

Genuine freedom emerges only when the 'I' is transcended, and the conflict is resolved in a state of mutual recognition. Each side then renounces the life-and-death struggle that had enslaved them and respects the reality of the other's will. Henceforth benefits are not commanded but *asked* for, and the condition of receiving them is the willingness to give in one's turn. In these new circumstances each party respects the will and autonomy of the other, renouncing the ways of coercion and acknowledging the other's rightful claim to respect. This is the condition that Kant summarized in his theory of the Categorical Imperative: the condition of 'respect for persons', in which people treat each other as ends in themselves and never as means only. In this condition people are genuinely free, since they receive the acknowledgement and respect that enables them to understand the value of the things they aspire to; they are in dialogue with other rational beings, and through that dialogue build a conception of a valid reason for action, a legitimate purpose, and an achievement that is worth the pursuit of it.

The price of this freedom is the price of reciprocity. I must acknowledge the rights and claims of others if I am to have rights and claims of my own. And as a free being I am accountable to others and can be called upon to justify what I do. Accountability and reciprocity inform all the ways of human society, and they are the foundation on which peace and happiness are built. Once we acknowledge this, however, we must also acknowledge that laws, customs, institutions and conventional constraints lie in the very nature of freedom. They are both the by-product and the channel of our reciprocal dealings. Moreover, they are not arbitrary or infinitely adjustable in the face of our desires but have a logic and structure of their own. In a social order founded on mutual recognition people retain their own goals and their own spheres of action. Their relations are governed by *constraints*, not shared purposes or imposed agendas. Hence outcomes are unpredictable, and arise by an invisible hand from dealings that do not intend them. This is quite unlike the situation of lordship, in which one party plans, decides and commands what is to happen. But, as I argue in Chapter Six, it is a fallacy to think that a society governed by plans and commands is better placed to predict, or in any way to guarantee, the outcomes desired. Moreover, it is only in a society governed by the 'invisible hand' that true equality can be achieved: not an equality of property, influence or power, but an equality of *recognition*, in which each individual is protected by his rights so as to be sovereign in the sphere that contains him.

This is not the place to develop all the philosophical ramifications of that argument. But it is important to grasp its central message. Life is valuable to us because *we* are valuable. Our value consists in our freedom and all that we accomplish by the proper use of it, in particular the *ordo amoris*, the order of love, which exists only where people confront each other from a position of responsibility. Freedom is genuine only when bound by the laws and institutions that make us accountable to each other, that oblige us to acknowledge the freedom of others and also to treat others with respect. Such laws and institutions have a core of universal morality – the 'natural law' of the Roman jurists and Aquinas, the 'moral law' of Kant or the 'Golden Rule' of Christian teaching, which tells us to do as we would be done by. They are also informed by historical experience, and evolve over time in response to the tensions and conflicts of human societies. In short, freedom belongs to individuals only by virtue of their membership in the 'we'.

Hence we are not born free: freedom is something we acquire. And we acquire it through obedience. Only the child who has learned to respect and defer to others can respect himself. And such a child is one who has internalized the rules, customs and laws that form the boundaries of a shared public world. Egotistic children who ignore those boundaries are at large in the public world, but have no real conception of it as public, as a place shared with others, whose respect and affection are the reward of good behaviour. They are not free in that world, but random, and the obstacles that others put in their path are a source of rage and alienation. Well-brought-up children have adopted as their own the constraints that make freedom possible. And this freedom is inseparable from the sense of the public validity and respect-worthiness of their own aims and projects.

All that should be obvious. But many people seem unable to take it on board. Perhaps the most vivid illustration of this lies in the revolution that swept through schools and departments of education during the 1950s and 1960s, and that told us, on the authority of a variety of thinkers from Rousseau to Dewey, that education is not about obedience and study but about self-expression and play. It was thought sufficient to liberate children from the constraints of the classroom and of the traditional curriculum, and they would express their natural creative powers, growing through freedom, and acquiring knowledge by explo-ration and discovery rather than 'rote learning'.[14]

A useful example of this fallacy is provided by the report of the Central Advisory Council on Education under Lady Plowden, delivered in 1967, and commissioned by the Minister of Education as guidance in the matter of primary schooling.[15] The growth of

14 Many trace the origin of 'progressive education' to Rousseau's *Émile*; John Dewey's *Education and Experience* appeared in 1938, and is the source of the view that education is either traditional and teacher-centred, or 'progressive' and 'child-centred'.

15 'Children and their Primary Schools', report of the Central Advisory Council on Education, chaired by Lady Plowden, London 1967. It should not be thought that progressive education emerged as a movement only in England and America. For the French experience, see Isabelle Stal et Françoise Thom, *L'école des barbares*, Paris, 1985.

'education' as an independent field of study, and the legislation that compelled new non-specialist teachers to attend a course in it, had produced a novel kind of 'expert', whose attachment to optimistic theories was not, as a rule, tempered by any prolonged experience of the classroom, or hindered by any special reserve of common sense. It was through the 'educationists' that the 'born free' ideology found its most potent channel of influence. Nothing served teachers better, in their new predicament as child-minders to the nation, than the vision advanced by the Plowden Report, with its 'proven' conclusion that education is a process of free exploration and self-development, in which the teacher plays the role not of expert, example or authority, but of adviser, playmate and friend. The net tendency of the Report was to suggest that the traditional methods – discipline, study and instruction – are of no particular value; indeed, that teaching itself is no part of the teacher's role. It warns us that 'a teacher who relies only on instruction... will disincline children to learn'. The teacher's duty is to stand by as the child expresses himself, eliciting but not controlling a response that is beyond judgement or reproach. If something goes wrong, then the child cannot be blamed – still less punished. Nor can the teacher be blamed, since his role is no longer that of initiator or guide. The only object of blame is 'society' and its hierarchies, and the 'deprived conditions' to which the school must offer a remedy. Where such abstractions are held responsible for failure, then only the state can provide the cure. The solution immediately adopted in the wake of the Plowden

Report was therefore exactly that which has been encouraged in the economic sphere by the best case fallacy: the subsidizing of failure, and the massive transfer of resources from those who make good use of them to those who do not.

In short, the born free fallacy leads by a series of natural steps to the two most important doctrines enshrined in the Plowden Report, which have become the foundations of educational policy in this country ever since: the doctrine that no party to the teaching process (neither pupil nor parent nor teacher) is to blame for its failure; and the doctrine that the state must invest in failure rather than success. Of course, the problems of education cannot be solved with a formula – certainly not when children are required by law to attend school, and subjected to the distracting noise of TV, internet and mobile telephone at all hours of the day. Nevertheless, it is a singular characteristic of the born free fallacy that it never considers the criticisms that have rendered it untenable to all moderately pessimistic people. Even if we are to ignore the arguments of Aristotle concerning the role of imitation, discipline and habit in the acquisition of character; even if we disregard the medieval philosophers (whose recommendations provided the indispensable foundations for the modern educational system); even if we ignore all that was said by Grotius, Calvin and Kant concerning the internal relation between freedom and law; even if we dismiss as antiquated every theory that does not place the idea of freedom at the centre of its vision – even if we do all that, a dose of pessimism would still persuade us that freedom, however valuable in itself, is not a gift of nature but the outcome of an educational process, something that we must work to acquire through discipline and sacrifice.[16]

Why this small dose of pessimism is never available in the minds of those who pursue the cause of 'liberation' is a question that has often troubled contemplative people, as it troubled Burke in his *Reflections on the French Revolution*. As the institutions of the French monarchy were one by one destroyed, and there arose, in the place of the liberation promised at the Revolution, a rapidly expanding terror, no remedy occurred to the Jacobins other than to cut off more heads. Each piece of evidence that the destruction of order was also a loss of freedom was interpreted in the opposite sense, as proof that things had not gone far enough. So destruction fed on destruction until, with Napoleon's coup d'état, the whole sorry process was brought to an end in a new form of civil order – but civil order imposed from above, and with the help of a nationwide military conscription.

The French Revolution is a vivid illustration of the way in which the fallacies of optimism renew themselves. This great event, which ought to have refuted the born free fallacy for all future generations, has been ever since reinterpreted as heralding the liberation of humanity from its oppressors. The very same fallacy can be read in subsequent calls to revolution by the Marxists, by Lenin and Mao, by Sartre and Pol Pot, for all of

16   That the lesson was not learned is conclusively shown by Chris Woodhead, *Class War: the State of British Education*, London, 2002.

whom the French Revolution was one step on the way to the goal of emancipation. And although Marx was intellectual heir to Hegel, and had the benefit of a philosophy that respected institutions and laws as the resolution, rather than the cause, of human conflict, he never ceased to believe in an original freedom – a freedom that was to be recaptured at the end of history, in the state of 'full communism' that would come about, when institutions were no longer necessary and the state would wither away.

The French Revolution is only one of the many historical events that show us that liberation movements, when they succeed in destroying the state, lead first to anarchy, then to tyranny, and in due course to totalitarian terror. But history has no lessons for unscrupulous optimists. All previous versions of their project, they believe, involved some fatal flaw – a conspiracy that usurped the liberating process and turned it in another direction. This escape route from refutation is made firmer and clearer by the 'utopian fallacy' and the 'zero sum fallacy' that I discuss in the next chapters. Even as it occurs, the destruction and desecration of human life that are the natural and indeed inevitable result of the born free philosophy are denied by the observing optimist – denied not because they have not yet been observed but because they are *unobservable*.

I had the opportunity to witness this in Paris in 1968, when my contemporaries were manning barricades, smashing cars and shops, assaulting policemen, and dressing in the obligatory denim uniforms of the new proletariat on the march. All of those whom

I knew among the participants in the *événements de mai* defined themselves as Maoists, carried the Little Red Book of inane maxims in their pockets, and heralded Mao's Great Proletarian Cultural Revolution as the model on which they were basing their own actions. They were confronting the 'fascist' state of de Gaulle, and the 'bourgeois' institutions through which it maintained itself in being. Now de Gaulle represented a party that had gained office by election; the institutions of the French Republic had been reformed and softened by nearly two centuries of history since Napoleon first imposed them; the Maoists themselves had enjoyed freedom, education and prosperity of a kind unimaginable in Mao's China. But all those facts were of no significance to the *soixante-huitards*. As for the tens of millions of victims of Mao Zedong, and the unspeakable sufferings that he inflicted on the peasantry whose interests he claimed to represent, such facts were unobservable. The slightest acquaintance with the available research would have shown the extent of the terror that Maoism had launched in China, but it was of no avail to point this out. The documents and reports were the work of 'bourgeois agents of influence'; those smuggled from China merely confirmed Mao's claim that 'reactionary elements' were conspiring to undo the work of the Revolution and the Great Leap Forward; the 'bourgeois' media were simply part of the false consciousness of French society, which prevented people from seeing the extent of their own enslavement; was it surprising therefore if the bourgeoisie viewed the Cultural Revolution with panic, and feared its spread across the world? Such was the only reasoned response I ever obtained when I protested at the destruction in which my contemporaries gleefully participated each day. In the chapter that follows I venture a partial explanation of this, in terms of another deep mental aberration, which I call the utopian fallacy. But, however explained, the failure of reason during the events of 1968 was entirely obvious to anyone who saw them from near at hand, and who had retained enough pessimism to permit the recognition of human folly.

At one level the 'revolution' of 1968 was a failure. None of the situationist, anarchist and new left movements came to power, and the institutions of the Western democracies remained more or less in place. At another level, however, the revolution was an astounding success. Many of those who took part in it either went on to occupy high political positions – like Oskar Fischer, Rudi Dutschke and Peter Hain – or played a major part in the cultural revolution that followed, and which was to dominate humanities departments in universities all across the Western world. This cultural revolution has taken many forms, but in every form, deconstructionist, feminist, counter-cultural or postmodernist, it retains the core agenda, which is to 'liberate' the student from the oppressive structures of the traditional curriculum, and also from the social institutions which that curriculum covertly endorsed.[17]

17 You can find the facts, somewhat intemperately summarized, in Peter Collier and David Horowitz, *Destructive Generation: Second Thoughts about the '60s*, New York, 1989.

At the heart of the new curriculum in the humanities, therefore, you will find the born free fallacy, ever fresh and ever creative, encouraging the destruction of any practice in which hierarchy, discipline and order have been enshrined, constantly promising 'liberation' to the 'real self' within.

Nor is the fallacy confined to academic circles. On the contrary, its greatest influence in our time has been in the development of new and optimistic versions of psychotherapy – versions that jettison entirely those sombre reflections on guilt and conflict contained in the work of Freud and his immediate disciples, and which instead emphasize the role of institutions in oppressing and confining the self.[18] During the sixties a psychotherapy of liberation arose, whose main theme was the natural freedom and authenticity of the self, and the role of institutions in eradicating that freedom and in typecasting the resulting protests as 'mental illness'. The inspiration was provided by Michel Foucault's *Histoire de la folie à l'âge classique* (1961), which argues that the madman is 'other' in what Foucault calls the 'classical age' because he points to the limits of the prevailing ethic and alienates himself from its demands. There is a kind of virtuous disdain in his refusal of convention. He must therefore be brought to order. Through confinement, madness is subject to the

---

18 Not that Freud should be exonerated entirely. His theories of infantile sexuality and 'repression' were pivotal in establishing the claims of liberationist psychotherapy. See Paul Vitz, *Psychology as Religion: the Cult of Self-Worship*, New York, 1977, second edn 1994.

rule of reason, itself to be understood as an instrument of domination in the hands of the rising bourgeois class. The madman is now defined by those whom he threatens, lives under their jurisdiction and is confined by their laws. The implication is that madness is an invented category whose purpose is not to help the madman, but to confine him, and to reimpose a moral order that he challenges. The next step is, of course, to suggest that he is right to challenge that order, that his madness is nothing more than an imposition by others, and that the real cure is to liberate him from their constraints, so that he can enjoy the primeval freedom whose call he has heard.

Foremost among the exponents of liberationist therapy was R. D. Laing, who took over from the French cultural revolution the wholesale assault on 'bourgeois' institutions, on behalf of the freedom that they supposedly deny. There is no such thing as mental illness, he argued, merely the disposition of some people to describe others as afflicted by it.[19] Labels like 'schizophrenia' are really weapons in a war of oppression, whose purpose is to shore up defunct institutions like the family against the pressure of a freedom that they cannot endure. 'Families, schools, churches are the slaughterhouses of our children,' he wrote. 'Colleges and other places are the kitchens. As adults in marriage and business we eat the product.'[20] Laing and his colleague Aaron

19 R. D. Laing, *The Divided Self*, Harmondsworth, 1960; R. D. Laing and Aaron Esterson, *Sanity, Madness and the Family*, Harmondsworth, 1964.
20 R. D. Laing, *The Politics of the Family and Other Essays*, London, 1971, p. 39.

Esterson took over Foucault's view that the bourgeois family creates madness as a way of destroying the original freedom that threatens it. The 'schizophrenic' is the one who is trying to hold on to his authenticity, his autonomous selfhood, against the 'double-bind' forced upon him by the family and its authoritarian demands.

The results of this particular application of the born free fallacy have been with us now for forty years. A dose of pessimism would have averted the long train of suffering that has followed the Laingian 'revolution' – suffering for patients, for their families, and for the community as a whole, which has had to live with policies that in some countries (notably the USA) have required hospitals to discharge their inmates on to the streets. One particular consequence – explored and deplored by Frederick Crews – has been the invention of 'false memory syndrome' and the supposed process whereby the 'victims' bring back into the sphere of memory the repressed traumas of child-hood abuse, from which they have never recovered.[21] In this way many resentful young people have dragged their parents into court, and even had them sent to prison, for entirely fictitious episodes of sexual molestation. This madness, too, proceeds from the born free fallacy, which supposes that the troubled psyche has been made that way by others, and that all children, left to them-selves, will express their freedom in wholesome and creative

---

21   Frederick Crews, *Follies of the Wise: Dissenting Essays*, New York, 2006.

ways. Indeed, it presupposes that children's faculties are already in place at the earliest age, enabling them to remember episodes that occur in the very first weeks of life – a presupposition shared by Freud in his theory of infantile experience and shown by recent developments in neuroscience to be untenable.

'False memory syndrome' is also a clear proof of the vindictiveness that is released when unscrupulous optimism comes up against the facts. Since it *must* be true that children are born free, any signs that freedom and autonomy have not been achieved must be blamed on others – and in particular on those nearest the child, who had the opportunity to stifle his development. In this way the born free fallacy feeds into another crucial fallacy of optimism – the fallacy that I discuss in Chapter Five, of seeing human relations as zero-sum games.

FOUR

The Utopian Fallacy

The two fallacies that I have discussed are so obvious and so easily avoidable that it is at first sight astonishing that anybody should commit them. Yet they have been at the root of the social and political movements that created the world in which we live, and the second of them – the born free fallacy – has dominated educational thinking throughout the twentieth century. How do we explain this?

That question can be answered, I believe, only if we have gone a little further into the weapons and shields that armour unscrupulous optimists in their war against reality. But one suggestion deserves consideration at this point, since it brings home the most important fact, which is that we are not dealing merely with local errors of reasoning, but with a *cast of mind*, and one that is in some mysterious way indifferent to truth. The suggestion is that the best case fallacy and the born free fallacy both belong to what the Hungarian philosopher Aurel Kolnai has called the utopian mind – a mind shaped by a particular moral and metaphysical need, which leads to the acceptance of absurdities not *in spite of* their absurdity, but *because* of it. According to Kolnai, the utopian mind is the central mystery of our times. It underlies the mass politics of Nazism and communism; it has infected the study of culture and society; and its dreams are continually recycled as 'solutions' to problems that they themselves create.[22] Kolnai's description of the utopian mind is close to that given of 'gnosticism' by Eric Voegelin – by which term Voegelin understood the tendency to import the transcendental directly into the real, and to demand that the 'final end' of the world be present here and now.[23] Voegelin thought of this as the primary religious heresy against which Christianity has battled since its inception on the Cross. And no doubt there is a tendency within every religion to embrace the absurd, as a kind of cancellation of this world and its imperfections. One explanation of utopianism, therefore, is as the residue of heresy in a world without religion. But it is at best a partial explanation, since it explains one way of clinging to absurdity in terms of another.

Although not everything that Kolnai says in his intriguing analysis is persuasive, he is right about one thing, which is that

---

22 Aurel Kolnai, *The Utopian Mind and other essays*, ed. Francis Dunlop, London, 2005.

23 Eric Voegelin, *The New Science of Politics*, Chicago, 1987. Voegelin's odd way of expressing this thesis has given rise to the popular cry 'Don't immanentize the eschaton' – in other words, don't try to build Heaven on earth.

utopians are not distinguished merely by a few beliefs that the rest of us are unable to share. They see the world differently. They are able to ignore or despise the findings of experience and common sense, and to place at the centre of every deliberation a project whose absurdity they regard not as a defect but as a reproach against the one who would point it out. This frame of mind has for two centuries played a leading role in European politics and none of the disasters that have stemmed from it has the slightest weight in deterring its new recruits. The millions dead or enslaved do not refute utopia, but merely give proof of the evil machinations that have stood in its way. This 'immunity to refutation' is what I mean by the utopian fallacy, and it is worth exploring it as one of the curious by-ways of optimism, and one that points the way to a *deep* explanation of why, in the human spirit, unreason is so endlessly renewable.

Karl Popper singled out the avoidance of refutation as the mark of pseudo-science, arguing that refutation is the backbone of scientific method and the way in which we rational beings negotiate life, 'so that our hypotheses die in our stead', as he famously put it.[24] But the utopian immunity to refutation is, I believe, immunity of a deeper kind than that which Popper discerned in the pseudo-sciences of his day. For it coexists with the knowledge that the utopia is impossible. Impossibility and irrefutability stand unembarrassed side by side.

24 Karl Popper, *Objective Knowledge: an Evolutionary Approach*, London, 1972, p. 248.

The best case fallacy arises when hope prevails over reason, in the presence of an important choice. It is not in itself utopian. Utopias are visions of a future state in which the conflicts and problems of human life are all solved completely, in which people live together in unity and harmony, and in which everything is ordered according to a single will, which is the will of society as a whole – the 'general will' of Rousseau, which might also be described, following the language of Chapter One, as a 'collective "I"'. Utopias tell the story of the fall of man, but in reverse: the prelapsarian innocence and unity lie at the *end* of things, and not necessarily at the beginning – although there is also a tendency to describe the end as a recovery of the original harmony.

Kolnai describes the utopian tendency as a 'hankering after some tensionless union of value and being'.[25] The desire is for a 'final solution', not just to one problem but to *problems as such*, so that whatever exists is compatible with what each person wants. All that creates tension and conflict is to be eliminated. Utopias differ according to their explanations of conflict. For some, conflict comes from power, and utopia is to be a condition in which no one has power over anyone else; for others, conflict comes from inequality, and utopia is to be a state of complete equality; for others still, conflict comes from private property, and will be overcome only in a world of common ownership. There are also utopias conceived along racial lines, like the Nazi

25   Op cit., p. 70.

'thousand-year Reich', which would be a condition of racial purity, with all alien elements removed. For the utopians of the French Revolution utopia would be a condition of 'liberty, equality and fraternity', a slogan that illustrates the aggregation fallacy that I discuss in Chapter Eight. In all its versions, however, utopia is conceived as a unity of being, in which conflicts do not exist because the conditions that create them are no longer in place. And invariably the conflict-creating conditions are described in ways that authorize violence – the violence needed to confiscate property, to enforce equality, to eliminate power, to destroy the cabals, conspiracies and alien races that prevent utopia from arriving.

The important point about utopia, however, is that it *cannot* arrive. There is no such condition as that alluded to, and a deep, if subliminal, knowledge of this fact prevents utopians from attempting a full critical description of the state they have in mind. Karl Marx's claim to have presented a 'scientific' as opposed to a 'utopian' socialism is a case in point. The 'science' consists in the 'laws of historical motion' set out in *Das Kapital* and elsewhere, according to which economic development brings about successive changes in the economic infrastructure of society, enabling us to predict that private property will one day disappear. After a period of socialist guardianship – a 'dictatorship of the proletariat' – the state will 'wither away', there will be neither law nor the need for it, and everything will be owned in common. There will be no division of labour and each person will live out the full range of his needs and desires, 'hunting in the morning, fishing in the afternoon, tending cattle in the evening and engaging in literary criticism after dinner', as we are told in *The German Ideology*. To say that this is 'scientific' rather than utopian is, in retrospect, little more than a joke. Marx's remark about hunting, fishing, hobby farming and lit. crit. is the only attempt he makes to describe what life will be like without private property – and if you ask who gives you the gun or the fishing rod, who organizes the pack of hounds, who maintains the coverts and the waterways, who disposes of the milk and the calves, and who publishes the lit. crit., such questions will be dismissed as 'beside the point', and as matters to be settled by a future that is none of your business. And as to whether the immense amount of organization required for these leisure activities of the universal upper class will be possible, in a condition in which there is no law, no property, and therefore no chain of command, such questions are too trivial to be noticed. Or rather, they are too serious to be considered, and so go unnoticed. For it requires but the slightest critical address to recognize that Marx's 'full communism' embodies a contradiction: it is a state in which all the benefits of legal order are still present, even though there is no law; and in which all the products of social cooperation are still in existence, even though nobody enjoys the property rights that hitherto have provided the sole motive for producing them.

That is one simple example of the contradictory character that informs all the utopias of our time. Those who advocate them rarely describe them, or touch on their nature only fleetingly in the course of denouncing the realities that impede their arrival. A case in point is Sartre who, in his later writings, moved increasingly in the direction of revolutionary utopianism, contrasting the 'seriality' (bad) of 'bourgeois' France with the 'totalization' (good) of the revolutionary future.[26] For Sartre the utopia will be a longed-for 'unity of intellectuals and the working class' to which he affords no description more exact than this: 'a concrete totalization continually de-totalized, contradictory and problematic, never closed back on itself, never completed, yet nevertheless one single experience'.[27] It is for the sake of utopia, so described – and described *explicitly* as contradictory, in mumbo-jumbo of a mind-boggling evasiveness – that Sartre justifies all the violence of revolution, and accepts, with a remarkable insouciance, the revolutionary necessity for a totalitarian state.

Sartre is indicative of the many utopians who have dominated intellectual life in Europe during the twentieth century. Like Marx, he denied that he was a utopian, and like Marx he gave only a shallow and contradictory glimpse of the future condition to which, however, he advocated absolute commitment. He leaped to the defence of revolutionary movements, and excused the ensuing violence and enslavement in familiar Jacobin terms. In an anthology published shortly after Sartre's death Marc-Antoine

---

26 See Jean-Paul Sartre, *Critique de la raison dialectique*, vol 1, Paris, 1960. Significantly vol. 2 of this work never appeared.

27 *Between Existentialism and Marxism*, tr. J. Matthews, London, 1974, p. 109.

Burnier gathered together the many instances of Sartre's revolutionary folly.[28] It is with a sombre incredulity that one reads of his support for exterminating regimes that unite the intellectuals and the proletariat only in the places of 're-education' where they gasp out their last miserable hours. 'By means of irrefutable documents we learned of the existence of actual concentration camps in the Soviet Union' – so Sartre wrote, twenty years after the truth was common knowledge among those who cared to recognize it. And yet still he could urge us 'to judge communism by its intentions and not by its actions', as though actions and intentions were as disconnected in tyrannies as they were in the mind of a café-haunting intellectual. In all the actual campaigns that the Soviet Union waged against the West, at whatever cost in human life and happiness, Sartre took the Soviet side, or else criticized the Soviet Union only in language that reiterated its own mendacities.

As I suggested, it is part of the appeal of utopia that utopias can never be realized. Those who espouse them are aware that final solutions are not available, that conflict and competition are essential features of human societies, and that all attempts to achieve a permanent unity of purpose or an absolute equality of condition are incompatible with the freedoms required by peaceful coexistence among strangers. Utopians must therefore live in a condition of constant preparation, fighting the enemies of

28 *Le testament de Sartre*, ed. Michel-Antoine Burnier, Paris, 1984.

utopia, and knowing that the fight will never end. In other words, utopia exists as a great negation sign, *un gran rifiuto*, to be affixed to everything actual and to command and authorize every form of violence against it.[29] Hence the utopian fallacy, which tells us that the ideal is immune to refutation. We need never turn back on our utopian aims, since utopia itself can never be realized and thus never disproved. It serves instead as an abstract condemnation of everything around us, and it justifies the believer in taking full control.

Many of those whose thinking is governed by the best case fallacy are pragmatists who do not seek the comprehensive reform of human society, but merely an enhancement of their own place within it. But the born free fallacy leads naturally in a utopian direction, since it makes a radical claim about the human condition, and uses that claim to destabilize the forms and conventions of our existing way of life. By identifying the essence of humanity with freedom, and freedom with a prelapsarian bliss, it urges people to destroy the 'structures' that stand in the way of a recovered innocence. It therefore has the same totalitarian tendency as the egalitarian doctrines of the Marxists.

Moreover, it leads naturally to the utopian fallacy. The ideal is contradictory and thus unachievable. And for that very reason it

---

29 'Vidi e conobbi l'ombra di colui/che fece per viltade il gran rifiuto' – *Inferno*, Canto 3. 'I saw the shade of the one who through cowardice made the great refusal'. We don't know to whom Dante was referring – maybe Pontius Pilate. But the accusation of cowardice is significant.

can never be refuted! No existing situation will ever qualify as a realization of that longed for and primeval freedom; so nobody will ever be in a position to say that we have achieved it, or to discover its damning faults. The ideal remains forever on the horizon of our experience, unsullied and untried, casting judgement on all that is actual, like a sun that cannot be looked at but which creates a dark side to everything on which it shines.

The most important criticism to be made of this way of thinking, it seems to me, is not that it is contradictory, though it is, but that, by pursuing a single and complete solution to human conflict, a solution that eliminates the problem forever, it destroys the institutions that enable us to resolve our conflicts one by one. I will return to this point in Chapter Six. But it is worth mentioning it now, since it is a point that was made by Burke in his great attack on the utopianism of the French Revolutionaries, and made again by both Chateaubriand and Tocqueville in their own more sober manner.[30] The solution to human conflicts is discovered case by case, and embodied thereafter in precedents, customs and laws. The solution does not exist as a plan, a scheme or a utopia. It is the residue of a myriad agreements and negotiations, preserved in custom and law. Solutions are rarely envisaged in advance, but steadily accumulate through dialogue and negotiation. They are a deposit laid down by the 'we' attitude, as it

30 Burke, *Reflections on the French Revolution*, 1790; François-René de Chateaubriand, *Mémoirs d'outre Tombe*, 1833, Book V; Alexis de Tocqueville, *L'ancien régime et la Révolution*, 1856.

unfolds through the norms of mutual dealing. And it is precisely this deposit, in customs and institutions, that the utopian sets out to destroy.

This is how we should understand the events of 1968 – events that irreversibly changed the political and cultural landscape of Europe and America and which brought into being a kind of institutionalized nihilism. The activists of 1968 were not in the business of perfecting the world. Their utopia was entirely constructed by negation, and such – I maintain – is the character of utopia in all its forms. The ideal is constructed in order to destroy the actual. And the 'liberation' from the structures that was demanded in 1968 was as much a self-contradiction as the 'concrete totalization continually de-totalized' of Sartre. It is summarized in the slogan 'il est interdit d'interdire' – an enforced forbidding of enforcement, the goal of which can never be defined.

Does this make the *soixante-huitards* into pessimists? Emphatically not. In my view they were the most unscrupulous of all optimists – unscrupulous in attacking the 'structures', optimistic in their conviction that by doing so they promoted their own and others' good. Like all such optimists, they could not be reasoned with. Nothing could be said that would confront them with the refutation of their ideal, for it was placed beyond refutation by its own impossibility.

In short, an unachievable goal chosen for its abstract purity, in which differences are reconciled, conflict overcome and mankind soldered together in a metaphysical unity, can never be questioned, since in the nature of the case it can never be put to the proof. All the crimes committed on the way to it are deviations, perversions or betrayals, things that the ideal was designed to prevent. In a strange way, therefore, the utopia is vindicated by the disaster of its implementation – the crime and the destruction could never be justified unless as stages on the way to some unquestionable good. It follows then that the ideal is every bit as pure as it claims to be. As for those who think it can be refuted by the facts, it is evident that they are guided by 'false consciousness', by a failure to see the world as it appears in the transfiguring light cast upon it by the utopian sun. The term 'false consciousness' comes from Marx and Engels, but it corresponds to the thinking of the French Revolutionaries, who saw all opposition to their schemes as a sign that the critic was an enemy of the people, just as it corresponds to the rejection of all criticism by the *soixante-huitards* as mere 'bourgeois' ideology, or as belonging to what Foucault called the *episteme* of the ruling class.[31]

But the utopian fallacy also reveals something important about optimism, in its extreme and uncompromising forms. For the person who entrusts all problem-solving to the single final solution, reality is without hope and without solutions. It must be forced into another mould, and to this end new forms of government and new, far-reaching powers will be needed. So behind the

31   Michel Foucault, *Les mots et les choses: une archéologie des sciences humaines*, Paris, 1966.

utopia there advances another aim altogether, which is the desire for revenge against reality.

Should utopians come to power, the very instability of their goal, which remains always out of reach, requires them to find, in the real world, the cabal or conspiracy that is preventing its realization. And this, to my way of thinking, is the most remarkable feature of totalitarian states: the constant and implacable need for a victim class, the class of those who stand in the way of utopia and prevent its implementation. In every totalitarian experiment, therefore, you will find that the first act of the centralized power is to single out certain groups for punishment. The Jacobins targeted the aristocracy, later expanded to the ubiquitous 'émigrés', whose invisible presence licensed the most arbitrary murders and exterminations. The Nazis singled out the Jews, on account of their material success and because of the ease with which they could be caricatured as 'Other'. The Russian communists began with the bourgeoisie, but were fortunate in having to hand another and more artificial class of victim: the kulaks, a class of property-owning peasants created by the state, which could therefore easily be destroyed by the state. By the time of the Moscow show trials, groups were being invented by the week to fill the role of sacrificial victim, as the utopian fallacy required. One function of the utopian ideology is to tell an elaborate story about the target group, showing it to be less than human, unjustly successful and intrinsically worthy of punishment. As I show in the next chapter, the schemes of the unscrupulous optimist quickly turn to retribution against those who dissent from them. And the most visible mark of dissent is the ability to fix your eyes on reality, and prosper nevertheless.

Hence totalitarian ideologies invariably divide human beings into innocent and guilty groups. Behind the impassioned rhetoric of the Communist Manifesto, behind the pseudo-science of the labour theory of value, and behind the class analysis against human history, lies a single emotional source – resentment of those who are comfortable with the ordinary world of human compromise, the world of the 'we', which stands in the way of the transcendental 'I' of the revolution. In order to destroy these people it is necessary to establish a militarized core to the state – whether in the form of a party, or a committee, or simply an army that does not bother to disguise its military purpose. This core will have absolute power and will operate outside the law. The law itself will be replaced by a Potemkin version, to be invoked whenever it is necessary to remind the people of the supreme goal that orders their existence. This Potemkin law will not be a shy retreating thing, like law in civilized societies, which exists precisely in order to minimize its own invocation. It will be a prominent and omnipresent feature of society, constantly invoked and paraded in order to imbue all acts of the ruling party with an unassailable air of legitimacy. The 'revolutionary vanguard' will be more prodigal of legal forms and official stamps than any of the regimes that it displaces, and the millions sent to their deaths will be granted an impeccable document to indicate that their end was rightfully decided and officially decreed. In this way the new order will be both utterly lawless and entirely concealed by law.[32]

The vanguard begins by targeting the culpable group, class or race. This will be a group marked by its previous success, the fruits of which will be taken from it and either destroyed or distributed among the victors. The members of the group will be humiliated and even reduced to some kind of animal condition, in order to display the extent of their former presumption. Hence the Gulag and the death camp arise naturally from the seizure of power. The camps convert their inmates into human rubbish, and therefore show them to be unworthy of the privileges that they previously enjoyed. The utopian impulse does not rest when its victims have been deprived of their worldly goods. It seeks to deprive them of their humanity, to show that they were never entitled to possess the slightest share in the earth's resources, and that their death is no more to be regretted than the death of any other kind of vermin. Exemplary in this respect was the humiliation of Marie Antoinette, Queen of France, who was accused of every crime, including incest, in order to represent her as excluded from the normal fold of humanity.[33] This humiliation of

32 Whittaker Chambers (*Witness*, New York, 1952) made the same observation of the communist cells in America and elsewhere under Soviet orders. Any crime could be permitted, but the piece of paper and the rubber stamp were an integral part of it, there being no distinction, in the last analysis, between permission and command.

33 See the tragic account of the Queen's destruction in Antonia Fraser, *Marie Antoinette*, London, 2001.

the victims is also a proof of the transcendental goodness of the hopes that they had prevented from being realized. In some way, which has more to do with religious than political ways of thinking, the sacrificial victim purifies the image of utopia; and the purification must be endlessly renewed.[34]

It is one mark of the utopian fallacy that it will not allow a right of reply. Those who are impeding the millennium bear their guilt on their face: it is because of their very existence that the utopia is being delayed. And utopians believe this, even though they know in their hearts that utopias are by their very nature 'delayed'. The gap between accusation and guilt is closed. Hence the importance of the new and often invented crimes, which signify an existential condition rather than a specific act of wrongdoing. 'You are a Jew/bourgeois/kulak.' 'Well, yes, I admit as much.' 'So what is your defence?'

However, the party that founds its rule on utopia will never feel at ease in the world that it creates. It will be like the puritan, as defined by H. L. Mencken, subject to 'the haunting fear that someone, somewhere, might be happy'. It will suspect that the refutation of utopia is already being discovered. Somewhere people are proceeding with the old way of life, expressing their energies, enjoying their successes, achieving the peace and

34 The religious aspect of this is brought out by René Girard, in *La violence et le sacré*, Paris, 1972, and *Le bouc émissaire*, Paris, 1980. Girard's thoughts are relevant to the case of Marie Antoinette, and I return to them in Chapter Ten, where their precise significance will, I hope, become apparent.

happiness that they are to enjoy only in that unreal future, when conflicts are transcended and mankind soldered into one. The ruling party will tirelessly search for the weeds of human industry, the first frail tendrils of ownership, the timid attempts of people to grow together in their 'little platoons'. It will never be certain that the émigrés, Jews, bourgeoisie, kulaks or whoever have been finally destroyed, and will be haunted by the sense that for every one killed another comes to replace him. It will be forced to confiscate not only the free economy but also the clubs, societies, schools and churches that have hitherto been the natural instruments of social reproduction. In short, utopia, once in power, will move of its own accord towards the totalitarian state.

Of course, the original utopians will die, most of them caught up in the machine that they made for others' destruction. One or two may even die from natural causes, though it is one of the pleasing lessons of recent history to discover how few they are. Eventually the machine will be functioning on automatic pilot, its software ossified into hardware. This is the final stage of totalitarianism – a stage not reached by the Jacobins or the Nazis, but reached in our day by the communists. In this condition, which Václav Havel ventured to call 'post-totalitarian', the machine runs itself, fuelled by its own impersonal distillation of the original idea. People learn to 'live within the lie', as Havel put it,[35] and go about their daily betrayals with routine acquiescence, paying their

35 'The Power of the Powerless', 1978, available in several collections of Havel's essays.

debt to the machine and hoping that someone, somewhere, might know how to switch it off.

The totalitarian extreme is not the only or even the normal consequence either of the best case fallacy or the born free fallacy. But its subliminal presence underlies another fallacy to which I now turn, one that illustrates how thin is the dividing line between unscrupulous hope and the vindictive desire to destroy hope's 'enemies'.

FIVE

The Zero Sum Fallacy

It is not only utopians who avoid disappointment by looking for the 'enemy within'. When committed optimists are faced with failure – either the failure of their schemes for themselves, or the failure of their schemes to improve the human condition – a process of compensation begins, designed to save the project by finding the person, the class or the clique that has thwarted it. And this person, class or clique is marked out for condemnation by the signs of success. If I have failed it is because another has succeeded – this is the strategic master-thought on which I can build the rescue of my hopes. This thought even has its equivalent among utopians, who know their hopes to be impossible and cherish them for that very reason. Even utopians feel the need to punish a world that has flourished without them, and whose success is thereby a rebuke to their failure to destroy it.

The thought can be expressed in another way: every loss is another's gain. All gains are paid for by the losers. Society therefore is a zero-sum game, in which costs and benefits balance out, and in which the winners' winning causes the losers' loss.

This 'zero sum' fallacy has been at the root of socialist thinking since the writings of Saint-Simon. But it achieved a classic statement in Marx's theory of surplus value. This purports to show that the profit of the capitalist is confiscated from his workforce. Since all value originates in labour, some part of the value that the labourer produces is taken by the capitalist in the form of profit (or 'surplus value'). The labourer himself is compensated by a wage sufficient to 'reproduce his labour power'. But the 'surplus value' is retained by the capitalist. In short, all profits in the hands of the capitalist are losses inflicted on the labourer – a confiscation of 'hours of unpaid labour'.

That theory does not have many subscribers today. Whatever we think of free market economics, it has at least persuaded us that not all transactions are zero-sum games. Consensual agreements benefit both parties: why else would they enter them? And that is as true of the wage contract as it is of any contract of sale. On the other hand, the zero-sum vision remains a potent component in socialist thinking, and a tried and trusted recourse in all the challenges offered by reality. For a certain kind of temperament, defeat is never defeat by reality, but defeat by other people, often acting together as members of a class, tribe, conspiracy or clan. Hence the unanswered and unanswerable complaint of the socialist, who will never admit that the poor benefit from the wealth of the wealthy. Injustice, for the socialist, is conclusively proved by inequality, so that the mere existence of a wealthy class justifies the plan to redistribute its assets among the 'losers' – a plan that exemplifies a further fallacy that I explore in the next chapter.

Not all optimists are socialists. Nevertheless, when plans are thwarted, consolation can be found in the zero sum fallacy, which says that wherever there is failure, someone is profiting from it. Perhaps the most important area in which this fallacy has been at work in recent years has been that of international relations, and in particular in the perception of the relations between the developed and the developing world, and it is worth considering the example, since it so clearly illustrates the way in which, and the typical circumstances in which, the zero sum fallacy is put to work.

It began in the immediate aftermath of the Second World War, when the Western powers had either lost their colonial possessions or were in the process of discarding them. The term 'Third World' or *Tiers Monde* was introduced by the demographer and economist Alfred Sauvy in 1952, and then politicized by Nehru in order to claim a common international identity for all those post-colonial countries that belonged to neither of the mutually antagonistic power blocs.[36] Since then the Third World has been treated as a single entity, and its social and economic disasters

36 Sauvy was expressly comparing the Third World with the 'Third Estate' on the threshold of the French Revolution: 'car enfin ce Tiers Monde, ignoré, exploité, méprisé comme le Tiers État, veut, lui aussi, être quelque chose'. *L'Observateur*, 14 August 1952 (paraphrasing L'Abbé Sieyès).

attributed to the relative success and tranquillity of the Western nations. 'Third worldism' has emerged as a systematic philosophy of excuses for the criminal conduct of post-colonial regimes. According to third worldists, the former colonies of the European powers need only to be liberated from the post-colonial relations of dependence, and provided with a large injection of capital in compensation for all that they suffered under colonial rule, and they will 'take off'. Some did eventually take off – notably India, Malaysia and the 'Asian tigers'. But many didn't, despite an immense investment of optimistic policy-making; and the function of third worldism was to fix the blame for this securely on the Western powers.

The Brandt Report of 1980 identified the problem in familiar zero-sum terms.[37] The 'South' (as the failures were called) was lagging behind because it lacked resources and could not match the spending power of the North. The solution was the Keynesian one of 'a transfer of resources from North to South'. This transfer, the Report argued, would stimulate the development of the impoverished nations and maintain their spending power, thus ensuring the survival of an international system that depended, in the end, on their ability and willingness to trade. Radicals rejected the Brandt Report as evidence of the cynical nature of international capitalism, which proposes to reform itself only for the sake of its own survival, and only in ways that will guarantee the

37 Report of the Independent Commission on International Development Issues, chaired by Willy Brandt, published New York, 1980.

persistence of the inequality upon which it depends.[38] Normal optimists accepted it as containing the solution to a problem that could be solved in no other peaceful way.

Already in 1971, however, a note of cautious pessimism had been sounded. P. T. Bauer and Basil Yamey argued that a transfer of resources to the Third World is harmful to both parties, serving merely to perpetuate local tyranny and to remove the local incentives to economic growth.[39] As they put it, 'to support rulers on the basis of the poverty of their subjects effectively rewards the policies which cause impoverishment'. The great Iraqi-born pessimist Elie Kedourie went further, arguing that 'national liberation struggles', when successful, mark not the beginning but the end of economic growth, and the extinction of the benefits conferred by colonial administration.[40] The arguments advanced by those thinkers may not be right – though subsequent history has led to their widespread acceptance, and their brave advocacy by Dambisa Moyo has made it easier for people to endorse them.[41] What is important, however, is that they involve a rejection of the zero sum fallacy, and a recognition that one agent's profit is not necessarily achieved through another agent's loss.

38 See, for example, Immanuel Wallerstein, *The Modern World System*, vol. 1, London and New York, 1974.

39 P. T. Bauer, *Dissent on Development*, Cambridge, MA, 1972.

40 Elie Kedourie, *The Crossman Confessions and Other Essays in Politics, History and Religion*, London, 1984.

41 Dambisa Moyo, *Dead Aid*, London, 2009.

During the last years of the millennium, on the other hand, the 'experts' in development economics were increasingly given to third worldism. Their view was either that the developing world would make economic progress, and wanted only help and 'pump-priming' from the richer countries; or that – if it was not making progress – this was largely due to the legacy of colonialism, which had prevented the formation of indigenous industries and markets. Not surprisingly, both positions were enthusiastically adopted by African leaders like Robert Mugabe, who eagerly held out their hands for subsidies while blaming the impoverishment of their people on the legacy of the colonial powers. The fact that the subsidies went into Swiss bank accounts on which the African leaders alone could draw was not regarded as particularly important by the experts. What interested them was the explanation of failure.

The zero-sum fallacy came to the rescue, not only of Mugabe and his kind, but also of the enthusiasts who had supported them. Failure in Africa was due to success elsewhere. The poverty of post-colonial Africa was the direct result of the wealth that the European powers had acquired through their colonies. In this way was perpetuated the doctrine that the people of Africa need not laws, institutions and education – as the colonial regimes had (in whatever rough and ready form) provided – but simply money, which would be just compensation for the assets the colonialists had seized. A completely inverted perspective thereby became orthodoxy. The Western powers were to cease providing the only thing that has ever been of the slightest benefit to Africa – namely government – and to provide instead the only thing that will guarantee the continent's ruin – namely money. In the nature of the case this money could be spent only in the West, rewarded corrupt elites and destroyed incentives for home production.

Third worldism is one of many examples in which the zero sum fallacy has been used to blame poverty on wealth, and so both to safeguard political illusions and to provide them with a useful 'enemy'. Indeed, perhaps the most interesting feature of the zero sum fallacy is its ability to support transferable resentments. If you injure me, I have a grievance against you: I want justice, revenge, or at least an apology and an attempt to make amends. This kind of grievance is between you and me, and it might be the occasion of our coming closer together should the right moves be made. The zero-sum way of thinking is not like that. It does not begin from injury, but from disappointment. It looks around for some contrasting success on which to pin its resentment. And only then does it work on proving to itself that the other's success was the cause of my failure. Those who have invested their hopes in some future state that will be one of blessedness will very often end up with transferable grievances, which they carry around, ready to attach them to every observed contentment, and to hold the successful to account for their own otherwise inexplicable failure.

Transferable grievances are normal among adolescents who, in their efforts to struggle free from family, church and school, will resent indifferently whoever and whatever makes some claim on their obedience. In the world of international politics, however, we discover that transferable grievances tend to focus on a common target – namely the United States of America, whose success in so many spheres attracts to it every kind of hostility from those who have failed in spheres of their own. This, it seems to me, is one of the causes (though, as I shall later argue, not the only cause) of anti-Americanism in our time. As the world's biggest economy, biggest military power, biggest source of faith, hope and charity, in worldly terms the biggest everything, America stands out as a target: it is manifestly 'asking for it'. Resentments that grow in out-of-the-way places, among people who have had no contact with America, will therefore quickly transfer themselves to this target, which is so large and so prominent that it cannot be missed. And the zero sum fallacy steps in to complete the argument.

The Greeks believed that, by standing too vividly above the mediocre level permitted by the jealous gods, the big man provokes divine anger – such is the fault of *hubris*. Believing this, the Greeks could enjoy guilt-free resentment. They could send their great men into exile, or put them to death, believing that in doing so they merely carried out the judgement of the gods. Thus the great general Aristides, who bore much of the responsibility for the victory over the Persians at Marathon and Salamis, and who was nicknamed 'the Just' on account of his exemplary and self-denying conduct, was ostracized and exiled by the citizens of

Athens. It is said that an illiterate voter who did not know Aristides came up to him and, giving him his voting shard, desired him to write upon it the name of Aristides. The latter asked if Aristides had wronged him. 'No,' was the reply, 'and I do not even know him, but I am tired of hearing him everywhere called "The Just".' After hearing this, Aristides, being just, wrote his own name on the shard.

Anti-Americanism does not have the kind of religious excuse that made resentment easy for the ordinary Athenian; but nor does it need it. Thanks to American freedom, every kind of wrongdoing can easily be discovered in America, and as easily publicized. Any crime needed for the anti-American case can be quickly unearthed and added to the indictment. And provided you eschew all comparative judgement, you need never become aware of the fact that your resentment accuses not America but you.

Wherever anti-Americanism flourishes, you will find some transferable grievance that avoids self-knowledge by this easy route. The anti-Americanism of the Eurocrats has everything to do with the failure of the European Union to inspire the loyalty that manifestly unites the American people, and next to nothing to do with America's presence in the world. The anti-Americanism of socialists has everything to do with the refutation of their philosophy by the American example, and next to nothing to do with the evils of American capitalism. In this connection there are few items of Marxist literature more comic than the writings of the Frankfurt school in exile – and in particular those of

Adorno and Horkheimer, who arrived in California to be confronted by the appalling sight of an unalienated working class. Adorno set about to dispel the illusion, producing reams of turgid nonsense devoted to showing that the American people are just as alienated as Marxism requires them to be, and that their cheerful life-affirming music is a 'fetishized' commodity, expressive of their deep spiritual enslavement to the capitalist machine.[42] In this way Adorno rescued a whole generation of Marxists from their predicament, by showing how to blame America for being a better place than their theory permits.

Anti-Americanism always finds new adherents, and the grievance that inspires them is itself always new. The anti-Americanism of the Islamists has everything to do with the stability that Americans enjoy and which has disappeared from the Muslim world, and little to do with the evils of American *jahiliyyah*.[43] Indeed, most Muslims in America live on peaceful and equal terms with people who do not share their faith, and cheerfully identify themselves as Americans. The sight of this is as outrageous to an Islamist as the sight of an unalienated working class was to Adorno. Islamists therefore express their resentment towards the Great Satan with a no-holds-barred antagonism that goes beyond even that of Adorno. But this should

42   See Theodor W. Adorno, *The Culture Industry: Selected Essays on Mass Culture*, ed. J. M. Bernstein, London, 1991.

43   The Islamic word for the condition of spiritual ignorance that the Prophet was sent to dispel.

not blind us to the fact that, like almost all the grievances that have finally come to focus on America, that of the Islamists has been transferred to this target from causes that have little or nothing to do with it. In the few years of its global rampage the Islamist grievance has targeted Hindus and Jews, heretics and apostates, democratic governments, peaceful communities, passengers on trains and buses, villagers who have lived by the *shari'ah* as well as the monks who have looked after them (the story of Tibhirine in Algeria).[44] It has targeted both the critics of Islam (Theo Van Gogh, Ayaan Hirsi Ali) and its friends (Naguib Mahfouz); and it has shouted with a loud self-righteous voice that Islam is a religion of peace (Tariq Ramadan), while daring you to suggest the opposite.[45] It has threatened the infidel with damnation while tearing itself asunder, as Sunni and Shi'ite dispute a right of succession that has no meaning whatsoever in the world we live in today. Islamism perfectly illustrates the way in which, by transferring your grievance, you can avoid the cost of understanding it, which is the frightening cost of self-knowledge.

This does not mean that the Islamic radicals are never right in their accusations. They hit the nail on the head about as frequently as Chomsky does, and to similar effect. And when they do so it is easy to agree with them. Who among us is entirely

---

44 See John W. Kiser, *The Monks of Tibhirine: Faith, Love and Terror in Algeria*, New York, 2002.

45 See Caroline Fourest, *Brother Tariq: The Doublespeak of Tariq Ramadan*, London, 2008.

pleased with the world made in America? Who among us does not wish that some kind of lid could be put on the licentiousness of the American culture machine? But that is not the point. A dose of judicious pessimism will remind us that there is an organic connection between freedom and its abuse, and that licentiousness is the price we pay for political liberty. Muslims want that liberty as much as we do: and to obtain it they migrate in their millions from the places where Islam is sovereign to the places where it is not – America being the final haven. And that is the source of the grievance. Radical Islam is cut off from the modern world: it interprets the revelation and the law as eternally fixed and unadaptable, and the sight of people successfully living according to other codes and with other aspirations is both a cause of offence and an irresistible temptation. Hence the Islamists make radical demands that are impossible to meet and which exist in order to affirm the identity of those who make them, rather than to invite a dialogue. And that, it seems to me, is the nature of much anti-Americanism in its current form: it is an existential antipathy, which cannot be met by any reform, since it is not a rational response to its target. It is the inverted recognition of failure.

The transferable grievances that have targeted America are now coming together in incongruous alliances that would be comic were they not so manifestly destructive. The radical ex-mayor of London, Ken Livingstone, whose worldview is a 'rainbow coalition' of resentments, welcomed with open arms both Hugo Chavez, the Venezuelan President, and Sheikh Yusef al-Qaradawi, the radical Egyptian cleric who has vowed the destruction of Israel; he embraced the activists of gay liberation, as well as the Mullahs who wish to execute them – all on the understanding that a shared antipathy to the traditional values of Western societies is sufficient to create common cause. The position of European leftists is indeed now fraught with paradox, as they find themselves allied against the 'American disease' with people who could at any moment take them as a target. As we know from the Nazi and Soviet experience, transferred resentments can change target at any time, and the best thing about them is their tendency to turn on each other.

Cautious people will ask themselves how best we might live in a world of transferred resentments. They may not agree with Nietzsche that *ressentiment* is the bottom line of our social emotions. But they will recognize its ubiquity, and its propensity to bolster its hopes and feed its venom through self-serving applications of the zero sum fallacy. It seems to me that there is no greater need for judicious pessimism than in confronting this fallacy, so as to prevent it from taking root in places where it can give to our basest emotions its spurious veneer of credibility. And the need is the more urgent in that zero-sum ways of thinking seem to emerge spontaneously in modern communities, wherever the effects of competition and cooperation are felt.

The zero sum fallacy has been of similar importance to that of the born free fallacy in justifying revolutionary politics. The

Russian October Revolution did not target Kerensky's government only. It targeted the *successful*, those who had made a go of things so as to stand out among their contemporaries. In every field and every institution, those at the top were identified, expropriated, murdered or sent into exile, with Lenin personally overseeing the removal of those whom he judged to be the best.[46] This, according to the zero sum fallacy, was the way to improve the condition of the remainder. Stalin's targeting of the kulaks exemplified the same cast of mind, as did Hitler's targeting of the Jews, whose privileges and property had in his mind been purchased at the cost of the German working class. The explosion of anti-bourgeois sentiment in post-war France, leading to works like Sartre's *Saint Genet* and Simon de Beauvoir's *Second Sex*, followed the same logic and was incorporated into the philosophy of the *soixante-huitards*.

Even without the context of revolution, zero-sum thinking has an important function in shoring up false hopes. One powerful example is the widespread belief that equality and justice are the same idea. Few people believe that if Jack has more money than Jill this is in itself a sign of injustice. But if Jack belongs to a *class* with money, and Jill to a class without it, then the zero-sum way of thinking immediately kicks in to persuade people that Jack's class has become rich at the expense of Jill's. This is the impetus behind the Marxist theory of surplus value. But it is also one of

46 For an account of one extraordinary episode, see Lesley Chamberlain, *The Philosophy Steamer*, London, 2006.

the leading motives of social reform in our time, and one that is effectively undermining the real claims of justice, and putting a spurious substitute in their place. It matters not that Jack has worked for his wealth and Jill merely lounged in voluntary idleness; it matters not that Jack has talent and energy, whereas Jill has neither; it matters not that Jack deserves what he has while Jill deserves nothing: for egalitarians the only important question is that of class, and the 'social' inequalities that stem from it. Concepts like right and desert fall out of the picture, and equality alone defines the goal. The result has been the emergence in modern politics of a wholly novel idea of justice – one that has little or nothing to do with right, desert, reward or retribution, and which is effectively detached from the actions and responsibilities of individuals. This novel concept of justice (which, I would maintain, is not a concept of justice at all) has governed educational reform in Western societies, particularly in Britain, where long-term class resentments have found a voice in Parliament and a clear target in schools. And the example is worth pondering, since it illustrates the near impossibility of escaping from zero-sum thinking when false hopes and transferred grievances feed on each other.

I came from a poor background and my parents had neither the ability nor the desire to spend money on my education. But I had the good fortune to gain entrance to our local grammar school, and thereby to work my way through the school to Cambridge University and an academic career. My grammar school, like many, had modelled itself on the public schools, adopting their curriculum, their style and some of their mannerisms. It aimed to provide its pupils with the very same opportunities that they might have had if their parents had been rich. And it succeeded. Those lucky enough to gain entrance to High Wycombe Royal Grammar School had an education as good as any then available, and the proof of this was that our old boys were represented among fellows of Cambridge colleges by a number second only to that achieved by Eton.

It was not justice to provide this opportunity to young people from poor backgrounds, nor would it have been an injustice to withhold it. The existence of the grammar schools arose from a long tradition of charitable institutions (my school was founded in 1542), which were eventually subsumed within the state educational system. But clearly a procedure that enables some pupils to succeed must cause others to fail: so the zero sum fallacy maintains. Such a procedure therefore generates a 'two-tier' education system, with the successful enjoying all the opportunities, and the failures left by the wayside to be 'marked for life'. In other words, the success of some is paid for by the failure of others. Justice requires that the opportunities be equalized. And thus was born the movement for comprehensive education, together with the hostility to streaming and the downgrading of examinations, in order to prevent the state education system from producing and reproducing 'inequalities'.

It is easy to ensure equality in the field of education: it suffices to remove all the opportunities for getting ahead, so that no child ever succeeds in learning anything. And to the cynical observer this is what happened. It is no part of my purpose to endorse that cynicism, though it has many times been expressed during the years since Anthony Crosland and Shirley Williams, education ministers under Labour governments, set about to destroy the grammar schools.[47] I wish simply to offer a stunning illustration of the zero sum fallacy at work. A system that offered to children from poor families an opportunity to advance by talent and industry alone was destroyed for the simple reason that it divided the successes from the failures. Of course, it is a tautology to say that tests divide successes from failures, and it can hardly be a requirement of justice to abolish that distinction. But the new concept of 'social' justice came to the rescue of the egalitarians, and enabled them to present their malice towards the successful as a bid for justice on behalf of the rest.

A dose of realism would have reminded people that human beings are diverse, and that a child might fail at one thing while succeeding at another. Only a diverse educational system, with well-designed and rigorous examinations, will enable children to find the skill, expertise or vocation that suits their abilities. Zero-sum thinking, which sees the educational success of one child as paid for by the failure of another, forces education into a mould

---

47 For example by Kingsley Amis and others in the 'Black Papers' on education, the first of which was *Fight for Education*, eds. C. B. Cox and A. E. Dyson, London, 1969.

that is alien to it. The child who fails at Latin might succeed at music or metalwork; the one who fails to get to university might succeed as an army officer. We all know this, and it is as true of educational procedures as it is true of markets, that they are not zero-sum games. Yet that is how they are treated whenever false hopes are invested in the utopian idea of 'education for equality'. The routine among politicians and educational experts is to hunt out places of excellence – Oxbridge, public schools, grammar schools, choir schools – and find ways to penalize them or to close them down. That way, the fallacy tells us, the others will benefit, and we will at last have an educational system that conforms to the requirements of 'social justice'.

In the penulitmate chapter I address the deeper question, how a cautious person might live in the world as we now find it – in which resentment assails us on every side, and in which the achievements and freedoms that we in the West enjoy are the target of a new and radicalized disappointment. But before returning to this theme there are a few more fallacies that I need to survey, in order that the reader may acquire a fuller picture of the abundant intellectual resources upon which people may draw, in rearranging reality to fit the shape of their hopes, and avoiding the difficult task to which reason calls them, which is to rearrange their hopes to fit the shape of reality.

SIX

The Planning Fallacy

Like the zero sum fallacy, the planning fallacy is not the peculiar property of optimists, and is prevalent wherever a certain kind of 'I' attitude takes over from the 'we'. It is the natural response to collective difficulties in the mind of anyone who does not recognize that consensual solutions to collective problems are not, as a rule, imposed but discovered, and that they are discovered over time. The planning fallacy consists in the belief that we can advance collectively to our goals by adopting a common plan, and by working towards it, under the leadership of some central authority such as the state. It is the fallacy of believing that societies can be organized as armies are organized, with a top-down system of commands and a bottom-up system of accountability, ensuring the successful coordination of the many around a plan devised by the few.

This fallacy has been effectively exploded in the sphere of economics by Mises, Hayek and other members of the Austrian school, and it is worth rehearsing their arguments before moving on to their wider application. These arguments began with the 'calculation debate', initiated by Mises and Hayek in response to socialist proposals for a centrally planned economy. The Austrian response to these proposals turns on three crucial ideas. First, each person's economic activity depends upon knowledge of other people's wants, needs and resources. Secondly, this knowledge is dispersed throughout society and is not the property of any individual. Thirdly, in the free exchange of goods and services, the price mechanism provides access to this knowledge – not as a theoretical statement, but as a signal to action. Prices in a free economy offer the solution to countless simultaneous equations mapping individual demand against available supply. When prices are fixed by a central authority, however, they no longer provide an index either of the scarcity of a resource or of the extent of others' demand for it. The crucial piece of economic knowledge, which exists in the free economy as a common possession, has been destroyed. Hence when prices are fixed the economy either breaks down, with queues, gluts and shortages replacing the spontaneous order of distribution, or is replaced by a black economy in which things exchange at their real price – the price that people are prepared to pay for them.[48] This result has been abundantly

48 The argument that I have condensed here is spelled out in detail in Ludwig von Mises, *Socialism: An Economic and Sociological Analysis*, tr. J. Kahane, London, 1936 (first published 1922 as *Die Gemeinwirtschaft: Untersuchungen über den Sozialismus*), and in the essays in Hayek's *Individualism and Economic Order*, London and Chicago, 1948, especially the three essays on 'Socialist Calculation' there reprinted.

confirmed by the experience of socialist economies; however, the argument given in support of it is not empirical but *a priori*. It is based on broad philosophical conceptions concerning socially generated and socially dispersed information. It is, in effect, a defence of the reasonableness of a real first-person plural, against the mere 'rationality' of the collective 'I' – a defence conducted in other terms by Burke on behalf of tradition against the 'reason' of the French Revolutionaries, and by Michael Oakeshott on behalf of civil association against the 'enterprise association' governed by plans and goals.[49]

The important point in the argument is that the price of a commodity conveys reliable economic information only if the economy is free. It is only in conditions of free exchange that the budgets of individual consumers feed into the epistemic process, as one might call it, which distils in the form of price the collective solution to their shared economic problem – the problem of knowing what to produce and what to exchange for it. All attempts to interfere with this process, by controlling either the supply or the price of a product, will lead to a loss of economic knowledge. For that knowledge is not contained in a plan, but only in the economic activity of free agents, as they produce, market and exchange their goods according to the laws of supply

---

49 Burke's target, in *Reflections on the French Revolution*, 1790, was the 'armed doctrine' of the Revolutionaries and their conception of goal-directed politics as required by Reason. Oakeshott's target, in *Rationalism in Politics*, London, 1962, was similar.

and demand. The planned economy, which offers a rational distribution in place of the 'random' distribution of the market, disrupts the information on which the proper functioning of an economy depends. It therefore undermines its own knowledge base. The project presents itself as rational; but it is not rational at all, since it depends on knowledge that is available only in conditions that it destroys.

One corollary of this argument is that economic knowledge, of the kind contained in prices, lives in the system, is generated by the free activity of countless rational choosers, and cannot be translated into a set of propositions or fed as premises into some problem-solving device. As the Austrians were possibly the first to realize, economic activity displays the peculiar logic of collective action, when the response of one person changes the information base of another. Out of this recognition grew the science of game theory, developed by von Neumann and Morgenstern as a first step towards an explanation of markets, but pursued today as a branch of mathematics with applications in every area of social and political life.

That powerful argument can be extended into other spheres – so as to justify, for example, the emergence of law through the common-law courts and the emergence of a health-care system through local charities and private hospitals. In every sphere where we have shared interests, and a need to cooperate, there is a difference between the order of the plan and the order of the invisible hand. Only rarely, and in special cases, does the order of the plan either meet its own requirements or obey the elementary principles of collective practical reasoning. Yet our world is increasingly subjected to the plans of bureaucrats and idealists, who suppose that they can present us with collective goals and then devise the means for reaching them. It is precisely in contemplating these plans that a dose of pessimism is most needed, in order to point out that no plan will stay in place for long, if people are free to disobey it, and that every plan will be thwarted, if its execution depends on information that the plan itself destroys. Conquest's Third Law of Politics tells us that the simplest way to explain the behaviour of any bureaucratic organization is to assume that it is controlled by a cabal of its enemies. This is a neat way of describing the normal result of the planning fallacy – that the thing intended will never be accomplished, and will very soon become irrelevant to those charged with achieving it.

It is obvious that the planning fallacy plays an important part in the utopian worldview that I described in Chapter Four. But it is by no means confined to utopians. Perhaps the greatest instance of the planning fallacy in our world today, and the most far-reaching piece of institutionalized folly that the free world currently witnesses, is the European Union, and it is worth examining this experiment in hope, which is a powerful illustration of the way in which, of their very nature, plans go astray by destroying the information needed to accomplish them. It seemed reasonable, even imperative, in 1950 to bring the nations of Europe together in a way that would prevent the wars that had twice almost destroyed the continent. And the new Europe was conceived as a comprehensive plan – one that would eliminate the sources of European conflict and place cooperation rather than rivalry at the heart of the continental order. The architects of the European project believed that the most effective means of creating the unity that they sought was through standardization imposed by a central authority, with the long-term goal of unification. This goal is invoked in all policy documents, as one that is inexorably advancing: an 'ever-closer union', by appeal to which every kind of law and regulation can be justified, as necessary parts of the plan. As a result, the nations of Europe are now snared in an expanding web of regulations that, by imposing crippling social and fiscal policies across the continent, erode the economic advantage that Europe would otherwise gain from its infrastructure and social capital.

The regime of standardization accompanies a new form of unaccountable quasi-government. Key decisions are taken by a small committee of national leaders. The task of translating these decisions into rules is assumed by a powerful administrative centre in which careers are pursued regardless of the plan, and in any case with no conception as to how the plan might be realized. At the same time the implementation of the rules is bequeathed to the Member States, along with the expense of complying with them. And the whole topsy-turvy process lies within the jurisdiction of a court that exercises its indeterminate powers in pursuit of the 'ever-closer union' that long ago ceased to be a realistic goal, but which can never be qualified or amended since it defines the contours of the plan.

Our continent is in a critical condition, economically, socially and culturally. State-dominated economies, committed to pension plans and welfare programmes that they can no longer finance; adverse immigration from minorities that do not accept either territorial jurisdiction or the elementary freedoms on which our political systems have been built; a loss of the Judaeo-Christian moral and spiritual inheritance, from which our law, our educational systems and our culture derive: in the face of these and many other critical developments the old project of integration seems, indeed, like a displacement activity, a way in which politicians busy themselves with illusory solutions, while hoping that the problems will go away. We saw this in the futile dither with which the European institutions responded to the catastrophe in Bosnia. We see it in the EU's much-hyped anti-terrorism strategy, the most concrete proposal of which is to create a 'non-emotive lexicon' for discussing the problem. We see it in the Commission's response to Russia turning off gas supplies to its neighbours, which is to 'complete the single market in energy' by building more interconnectors. The whole process of regulation and dictatorship seems to be adrift in cloud-cuckoo land. Yet it is an impeccable product of the plan, and of the top-down method of implementing it.

The effect of the planning fallacy is best seen by studying the attempts to counter its centralizing effect. These attempts focus on the term 'subsidiarity'. This word, incorporated into the Maastricht Treaty and ostensibly guaranteeing local sovereignty, is a term of Roman Catholic social thought, and was given its current sense in an encyclical of Pope Pius XI in 1929.[50] According to Pius XI, 'subsidiarity' means that decisions should be taken always at the lowest level, by groups and communities that themselves take charge of the matters decided.

The term was appropriated by Wilhelm Röpke, the German economist who, exiled from Nazi Germany in Switzerland, was amazed and impressed to discover a society that is the opposite in so many ways to the one from which he had escaped.[51] He saw that Swiss society is organized from the bottom up, and resolves its problems at the local level, through the free association of citizens in those 'little platoons' to which Edmund Burke had made such passionate appeal when decrying the top-down dictatorship of the French Revolution. Subsidiarity, in Röpke's understanding of the term, refers to the right of local communities to take decisions for themselves, including the decision to surrender the matter to a larger forum. Subsidiarity places an absolute brake upon centralizing powers by permitting their involvement only when requested. It is the way to reconcile a market economy with the local loyalties and public spirit that it might otherwise erode. It is, in short, the name for an economy that places 'we' before 'I' and

---

50 *Divini illius magistri*, Vatican, 1929.

51 Wilhelm Röpke, *A Humane Economy: the Social Framework of the Free Market*, London, 1960.

recognizes that social and economic order emerge from our tacit bargaining as by-products and not as goals.

In the EU as it is today, the term 'subsidiarity' denotes not the means whereby powers are passed up from the bottom, but the means whereby powers are allocated from the top. It is the EU and its institutions that decide where subsidiary powers begin and end, and by purporting to grant powers in the very word that removes them, the term 'subsidiarity' wraps the whole idea of decentralized government in mystery. For the Eurocrats, national governments are autonomous only at the 'subsidiary' level, with the European institutions uniquely empowered to determine which level that is. This is precisely what the planning fallacy requires: all decisions are legitimate, save those that run counter to the plan. And only the guardians of the plan know what those decisions are.

But the goal of the plan, meanwhile, slips from view: who knows how to achieve the 'ever-closer union' that is the liturgical frame of EU documents, what it would look like if we achieved it, or whether its most ardent advocates would still wish to promote it, once they had seen it face to face? The empty phrase can be translated into nothing cogent save more laws, more rules, more government, more power to the centre. The result is a large-scale loss of the information – information about people's wants and needs and loyalties – on which the implementation of the plan would depend. The plan destroys its own knowledge-base.

Without venturing too far into political theory, it is surely not contentious to assert that, if there is a reason above all others to praise the civilization of Europe, it lies in the emergence on this continent of a rule of law, in which law stands higher than those who make it and holds them to account for what they do. The 'empire of laws, not of men' was no innovation of John Adams, but an ideal already defended in the *Politics* of Aristotle, an ideal implicit in the *Institutes* and *Digest* of Justinian, and one to which the thinkers of the Middle Ages and the Renaissance returned again and again.

It is precisely for this reason that law, in Europe, has been connected with national sovereignty. Law, for us, is the law of the land. And although many of our legal systems derive in large measure from what was, originally, the universal jurisprudence of Roman law, they have evolved in different ways in different places, and incorporated into themselves the legacy of national history. It should be remembered that the laws that survive in any state are not those made in times of war or other emergency, but those made in times of peace. The legal systems of Europe contain within themselves – and especially in what pertains to civil association – the legacy of peace, and the formula for re-establishing peace after any conflict. To interfere with their operation, or to override their provisions with edicts that are not responsive to the deep sediments of argumentation that they contain, is to put at risk the most important source of stability in the European communities.

But it is precisely in its approach to law that the planning fallacy enshrined in the European project has proved most destructive. The common law of England conforms to the model of collective rationality that Hayek calls 'catallactic'.[52] It is not imposed from above by some executive body, but constructed from the bottom by discovering the just solutions to real human conflicts, and then deriving from them, through the doctrine of precedent, a system of legal rules. Our law is binding on the sovereign, since it consists in the remedies that the courts have offered in the sovereign's name; and it can avoid unjust edicts through the 'doctrines of equity', which produce those marvellous intellectual constructs such as trust, beneficial ownership and injunction, which – on some understandings – are responsible for the pre-eminence of England in the world of finance. In all kinds of ways the common law resists dictatorship, and even if it is also a rule of common law that the courts apply all statutes according to 'the will of Parliament', it is for the courts, not Parliament, to discern what that will might be. Furthermore, the rootedness of the common law in the search for remedies has meant that it responds immediately to grievances, and has made the top-down regulation of commerce largely unnecessary. Product liability, for example, governed in continental systems by massive regulation, was, until entry into the European Union, largely governed in English law by the leading case of *Donoghue* v. *Stevenson* of 1932, in which someone made ill by a decomposed snail that had found

52   F. A. Hayek, *Law, Legislation and Liberty*, 3 vols, London, 1973, vol. 1.

its way into a ginger-beer bottle successfully sued the manufacturer. The case made it clear that the rule of common law is not, as in Roman law, *caveat emptor*, but rather *caveat vendor* – let the vendor take note of his duty of care towards all those who can reasonably be expected to encounter his product.

The legislative powers conferred on the Council of Ministers by the Treaty of Rome were not intended at the time to issue such a flood of edicts as to become responsible for most of the legislation adopted by the assemblies and parliaments of the Member States. Yet that is what has happened and, not surprisingly, the common law sits uneasily with this kind of machine-made law. It goes entirely against the grain of English jurisprudence to believe that an edict issued from Brussels is *already* part of the law of the land, even before it has been discussed in Parliament or tried in the courts. And it is not only the common law of England that bridles against this top-down approach to legislation. The laws of the European states are either discovered, like the common law, in the intricacies of social conflict, or adopted by elected assemblies after open discussion and the published deliberations of committees. In all the national systems of law the attempt has been made to fit law to the perceived social needs of the nation, and to solicit the consent of the people not merely law by law but case by case, through the workings of the courts. By contrast, the edicts of the Council of Ministers are issued after unminuted discussions held in secret, on the basis of proposals made by the bureaucrats of the

Commission, guided by principles in which the limits to legislation are not clearly stated or publicly rehearsed. Yet, under the doctrine of 'shared competence', it is held that where the EU and a Member State both have the right to legislate in a certain area, the Member State's right ceases just as soon as the EU decides to exercise its competence.

The problem here lies deep within the structure of the European Union. Laws passed as a result of EU regulations are not merely adopted by the legislatures of the Member States. They are effectively subsumed under the Treaties, and therefore made irreversible. The most basic rule of law-making – that mistakes can be corrected – is absent from the European legal process. At the same time the European Court of Justice, which is supposed to rule on all conflicts created by the European legislation, is expressly called upon to advance the project of 'ever-closer union', and will therefore, in any case where judicial discretion or innovation is needed, look to that project for its guiding principle. This is, indeed, required of it by the EU's doctrine demanding the 'sincere mutual cooperation' of institutions within the Union.

The irreversible quality of EU legislation is already implied in the term – the *acquis communautaire* – used to describe it. This term denotes the entire body of laws, policies and practices that have at any given time evolved within the EU; but it refers especially to those laws and procedures in which the central apparatus has acquired powers previously exercised by the Member States, and henceforth to be exercised by the Union. Only with the

Maastricht Treaty of 1992 did the term become part of the official terminology, but some years before then it had been clear that the *acquis* exists, that it is the real and lasting achievement of the Union, and that it obliges Member States to accept all previous and future centralizing measures, while implicitly ruling out the repatriation of any acquired powers. The written laws, regulations and procedures of the *acquis* now amount to over 170,000 pages; few experts have knowledge of much more than a tiny part of it. And to go from page to page, examining the thousands of fussy regulations and the often malicious confiscations of democratic authority, is to receive an impression of meddlesomeness verging on the insane. This impression is as common among believers in the project of 'ever-closer union' as it is among the advocates of subsidiarity. Almost everyone seems to agree that something has gone wrong; that a machine has been put in place that lacks some of the gears necessary to its proper functioning.

If you look back at the Russian Revolution, and all the disasters that flowed from it, from the liquidation of the kulaks, through the Ukrainian genocide and the Nazi-Soviet pact, to the final grim routines of the Gulag-tormented state, you will surely ask yourself what went wrong that each mistake should be followed by a larger one. The answer is plain. By abolishing all the institutions through which the Party and its members could be held to account for what they did, Lenin destroyed the means whereby mistakes could be rectified. His one-party state, governed by plans imposed from above, was a machine without feedback that was no sooner in motion than it was out of control. Something similar has happened in the European Union. Of course, the goals are less ignoble and the results more benign. Nevertheless, there seem to be few if any ways in which mistakes can be rectified or the people who make decisions held accountable for the results of them. The *acquis* is a sure proof of this. It is always growing, and no addition to it is ever lost.[53] However foolish it may be for the European institutions to take charge of some matters best dealt with by the Member States, no power, once transferred, is ever recaptured. Ridiculous regulations can be duly laughed at from top to bottom of the Union; but the laughter rings hollow, since it meets with no response. A cavernous void lies at the heart of the European process, a void into which questions are constantly called out by the people, and from which no answer ever returns.

Laws that, once accepted, become subsumed under a treaty are laws of a radically different status from laws passed by a normal legislative assembly. When a national assembly passes a bad law, a subsequent assembly can repeal it: no procedure is required to undo the mistake other than the one that first produced it. But the

53 According to the generally reliable think tank Open Europe, the number of legal acts in force in the EU has risen from 10,800 in 1998 to 26,500 in 2008; the annual cost of regulation on the UK has gone from £16.5 billion in 2005 to £28.7 billion in 2008, while the cumulative cost of regulation over the ten years to 2008 was £148.2 billion – 10 per cent of GDP. Seventy-two per cent of that cost was due to EU regulations. Report issued March 2009.

peculiar nature of European law forbids this simple process of rectification. Law, once made, is taken out of the sphere of discussion and insulated from repeal by its status under the Treaties. Since no Member State will contemplate repudiating the Treaties, at any rate for so simple a matter as an irksome regulation or even a large but bearable financial cost, bad laws remain on the books, buried in the 170,000 pages of the *acquis communautaire*. These laws, which tie the hands of the European states and are making Europe as a whole increasingly less competitive in the world economy, are also bringing the entire legislative process into disrepute. In due course the habit of disobedience will become so widespread that the people of Europe will consider themselves as little bound to obey the European Commission as the Commission feels bound to account to the people. When that happens the Union will be at an end; but it may happen too late, and after the kind of continent-wide collapse that many commentators are now predicting. Far better, surely, to listen to the pessimists now and stop planning for an 'ever-closer union'.

As Lenin illustrated, the worst kind of government is not that which makes mistakes, but that which, while making mistakes, is *unable to correct them*. When the powers of government are properly divided, and when those with sovereignty can be ejected by a vote, mistakes may find their remedy. But suppose the institutions of government are set up in such a way that all concentration of power is irreversible, so that powers acquired by the centre can never be recaptured. And suppose that those who rule at the centre are appointed, cannot be removed at popular request, meet in secret and keep few or no minutes of their decisions. Do you think that, in such circumstances, the conditions exist in which mistakes can be rectified, or even cogently confessed to? Look at the public pronouncements of the European Commission and try to find evidence of contrition, and you will look in vain. Following the 'no' votes of the French and the Dutch respecting the Constitutional Treaty, the EU and the government of France launched websites designed to prove that the people have always been consulted. But the websites are one continuous stream of propaganda, conveyed in the kind of Eurospeak that, like Orwell's Newspeak, makes heretical thoughts inexpressible. Likewise, the 'no' vote of the Irish people to the Lisbon Treaty elicited nothing more than a request to vote again. Furthermore, look at the treaties and their accompanying propaganda, and you will find only imperatives, timetables, declarations of what *must* be achieved by *when*, rather than appeals for popular consideration and open debate. In short, there is no plan B, no means of reversing decisions once made, no way of allowing a voice to the 'we' against the torrent of edicts from a crazed collective 'I'.

The planning fallacy leads to another: the disaggregation of problems. In order to proceed towards our collective goal we must address each issue from the same central standpoint. If a problem arises that needs solving then we solve it through a regulation. But solving one problem gives rise to others, which – because they belong to another department or lie in the future –

are not considered by the legislative machine. Moreover, nothing authorized by the plan can be reversed. So we are saddled with the EU Directive for Personal Protective Equipment 89/696, which requires Wellington boots to be sold with a 24-page user's manual in ten languages, giving advice on risk assessment, storage conditions, life expectancy, washing in a mild detergent, and resistance to electricity, cold weather and oil (though not water). Users are advised to try each boot for fitting before use, and even the amount of energy absorbed by the heels is recorded. The manufacturers are required to test their boots twice a month at EU-approved laboratories to ensure that they comply with standards. And so on. The top-down approach means that the legal instruments, whether in the form of Regulations, Decisions or Directives, are prepared by a busy army of bureaucrats within the European Commission, rather than by elected representatives of the people. These bureaucrats suffer no penalty for their mistakes, are unknown to the people, and cannot be removed from office by those whom their decisions affect. Their business is to regulate; if ever it were decided that no more Regulations are needed, there would be no further use for them, except to police the surviving edicts. Hence, following the logic of Parkinson's Law — as confirmed by the public choice theory of rent-seeking[54] — the bureaucrats of the Commission seek to expand the reach and

54 James Buchanan, 'Rent-seeking, Non-compensated Transfers, and Laws of Succession', *Journal of Law and Economics*, April 1983, pp. 71–85; *Cost and Choice: An Inquiry in Economic Theory*, Indianapolis, 1999.

number of their products, and to recruit as many helpers as possible in their efforts to augment the pile.

The unstoppable nature of European regulation is enhanced by two further factors. The first is the lack of any constitutional limitation on what can and what cannot be the subject-matter of a Regulation. Many matters fundamental to the identity of the local and national cultures of Europe have already been subjected to central regulation, and the legislative machine is such that scrutiny by national Parliaments may be entirely ineffective in preventing the regulation from taking effect. A case in point is the abolition of traditional British weights and measures by edict from Brussels. Customs fundamental to the day-to-day transactions, the history and the culture of the British people were abolished without compunction by bureaucrats who would listen to no protests, since listening to protests is no part of their job. As from 2010 there is to be a total ban on the marketing of goods within the EU using non-metric measures. This regulation will make it impossible for British firms to market their products in the many countries in the Anglosphere (the USA for instance) where imperial measures are still in force, except by packaging them in two separate formats – an impossibly costly procedure for many small businesses, and an impertinent affront to customs rooted in national history. In similar manner 'health and safety' measures have destroyed local markets, filled the environment with non-degradable plastic packaging, and prevented the small farmers of Romania from selling their produce at the gate of the farm, since

EU regulations insist on the packaging of agricultural products. (This last regulation, if followed to the letter, will mean the end of traditional Romanian agriculture, and the surrender of that still beautiful countryside to agribusiness – a sad return to the peasant farmers who were the backbone of their country in the years of Ceauşescu, and also the target of his own insane and vindictive applications of the planning fallacy.)

In all its forms planning has a dangerous tendency to ignore the way in which, by the law of unintended consequences, the solution to one problem may be the start of another. In an elected and accountable legislature, with open and transparent committees and full scrutiny by the press, voices from beyond the chamber can point out the undesirable side-effects of legislation, and urge that they be taken into account. This does not happen, however, when regulations are imposed by a plan. Two far-reaching examples will illustrate what I mean. Since 1996 the EU has issued a series of Directives on air quality, limiting the size and quantity of dust particles in the air. These Directives, passed into Dutch law in 2001, require concentrations of dust so low that they could not be achieved in a densely populated country like the Netherlands, where in any case sea salt and soil clouds constitute 55 per cent of the atmospheric dust content, and two-thirds of the remainder is blown in from abroad. Nevertheless, the law has been enforced, bringing a large number of building projects to an end, including roads, industrial parks and housing projects in the centre of Amsterdam, since the ambient dust levels surpass what is permitted for places in which people are to live or work. Epidemiological studies indicate that, thanks to atmospheric dust, 'the lifespan of some thousands of people is reduced by a few days to a few months'. Despite this, Environment Commissioner Stavros Dimas insists on yet more stringent regulations, to be put in place in 2010 and 2015, arguing that delays in reaching the chosen targets 'would be playing with people's lives'. That it might be playing rather more seriously with people's lives to fail to provide the housing required to shelter them or the industry required to employ them is not a relevant consideration: for those things belong to another department, and the essence of bureaucratic regulation is that it proceeds problem by problem and neither needs nor is able to take account of the whole.

The second case concerns a European Directive issued in response to the slight risk that diseased animals might enter the human food-chain, and which insists that all slaughter should now take place in the presence of a qualified vet, who must inspect each animal as it arrives at the abattoir. There is no evidence that veterinary examination in these circumstances is either necessary or (in the rare cases when infected animals come to the abattoir) effective. Nevertheless, the Directive was issued and passed into British law, with disastrous consequences.

Veterinary qualifications are hard to obtain in Britain, with the result that vets demand high fees for attendance. Small abattoirs all over the country were therefore forced to close down, since their profit margins are as narrow as those of the farmers whom they serve. The effect of this on husbandry, on the social and economic life of farming communities, and on the viability of small pasture farms, has been devastating, the effect on animal welfare equally so. Instead of travelling a quarter of an hour to the local abattoir, herds must now travel three or four hours to one of the great processing plants that enjoy the presence of a permanent vet. Farmers who have taken pride in their animals and cared for them through two or more winters are distressed to part with them on such terms, and the animals themselves suffer greatly. This damage done to the relationship between farmer and herd has further adverse effects on the landscape. Unable to take full responsibility for the life and the death of his animals, a farmer ceases to see the point of his unprofitable trade. The small pasture farms that created the landscape of England are now rapidly disappearing, to be replaced by faceless agribusinesses or equestrian leisure centres, and the EU has contributed in no small measure to this decline.

As if those long-term costs were not bad enough, the British have also had to endure the short-term cost of foot and mouth disease, which in the past would usually be contained in the locality where it broke out. In its latest occurrence the disease was immediately carried all over the country by animals on their way to some distant abattoir. The result was the temporary, but total, ruination of livestock farming.

Now elected politicians would have taken into account not only the small risk addressed by such a Directive, but also the huge risks posed to the farming community by the destruction of local abattoirs, the risks posed to animals by long journeys, the benefits of localized food production and local markets for meat, and so on. And they would have had a motive for considering all those things, namely their desire to be re-elected, when the consequences of their decision had been felt. As rational beings they would recognize that risks don't come in atomic particles, but are parts of complex organisms, shaped by the flow of events. And they would know in their hearts that there is no more risky practice than that of disaggregating risks, so as one by one to forbid them. Even bureaucrats, in their own private lives, will take the same line. They too are rational beings, and know that risks must be constantly taken and constantly weighed against each other. However, when bureaucrats legislate for others, and suffer no cost should they get things wrong, they will inevitably look for a single and specific problem, and seize on a single and absolute principle in order to solve it.

In the face of the absurd and intrusive regulations, it is a normal and understandable response to demand more 'accountability' from those who generate them, and from those who push forward the ever-accelerating journey to nowhere that is the refrain of official documents. And of course, if we could secure accountability for every aspect of the European process, many of the justified complaints of the European people would be answered. But what is accountability and when does it occur? An officer is accountable for his official actions only if those whom his office serves have a remedy against his abuse of it. And it is precisely this that is lacking in the European institutions, which have been set up with peremptory speed and without regard to the conditions that might generate their popular acceptance. An obvious instance is provided by the Commission itself. No accountant has been able to pass unqualified accounts for the Commission for the last twelve years; the evidence of massive corruption and negligence is overwhelming; and popular discontent with this fact is constantly recorded in the press. Yet there is no sequel, apart from the censure of the accountant, or the persecution and dismissal of those 'whistle-blowers' who have dared to report on the Commission outside its fortified walls. It is true that, in the wake of one astonishing scandal, the Commissioners all resigned. But they promptly reappointed themselves, since both the resignation and the reappointment were decisions governed entirely by themselves, and the people had no say in them. This episode, which might appear at first glance to be proof that the Commissioners are, in some way, accountable, is in fact clear proof of the opposite: no one can control them but themselves. At the root of the planning fallacy lies the problem identified two millennia ago by Terence: *Quis custodiet illos custodes?*

And here we see why the so-called 'democratic deficit' in the European institutions is a built-in feature of them. The institutions were set up in such a way that they could be influenced from below, but controlled only from above. Accountability, however, means influence from above, but control from below – control by those whose interest is served, and who retain the ultimate remedy of ejection. True subsidiarity means that those who surrender their powers to some higher court or parliament retain the ability to eject its officers for abuse of those powers. This ability is presupposed in the modern idea of citizenship, which views the powers of government as conferred by the consent of the citizens, a consent that can be withdrawn at an election. This kind of control from below (which is what we mean, or ought to mean, by democracy) is not easily achieved, and was achieved in Europe only at the end of a long and painful process of nation-building. The nation-state offered to its members a common loyalty, a way of envisaging their togetherness, which made the project of electing and ejecting their representatives intelligible to the ordinary citizen. Thanks to national loyalty citizens were able to set religion, family and personal networks in the background of politics, and make common cause with strangers in the election of their government. They were able to acquire that strange habit – unknown in most of the world – of regarding people whom they intensely disliked and would never vote for as nevertheless entitled to govern them. Bound together by ties of nationhood, and trusting the political process that gave ultimate control to the citizens, the members of nation-states have been able to create institutions that hold their leaders and representatives to account for everything that affects the common interest. The nation-state is the unplanned expression and by-product of a consensual process. And it is for this very reason that it is offensive to those who live by the plan.

I have dwelt at length on the European Union since it is a clear illustration of the general point that – at the level of society – the outcome of a comprehensive plan can never be foretold, and the pursuit of the plan regardless involves a kind of wilful blindness to reality. But what is the alternative when societies enter into periods of conflict and catastrophe of the kind that destroyed the peace of Europe? Surely the reasonable view is that we should aim for a social order based on constraints, not on goals. In this context the medievals wrote of the 'natural law' – the constraints that all of us are guided by, just so long as we allow the voice of reason to sound in our affairs and are prepared to renounce our goals in obedience to it. Grotius hoped to turn this natural law into a system of international jurisdiction, which would bring belligerence to an end by providing a universal standard in the affairs of nations, enabling them to resolve their disputes in a peaceful manner. Kant reformulated the idea in terms of his 'categorical imperative', which does not tell us what we should aim at, but only what to avoid. We must act on 'that maxim which we can will as a universal law' – Kant's equivalent of the Jewish and Christian Golden Rule that tells us to do as we would be done by. The categorical imperative provides a test that our principles and aims must pass, if we are to adopt them. It does not determine what those principles and aims might be, but establishes the constraints within which we may reasonably pursue them. As such it lays the foundations for cooperation between free and rational beings, and ensures that, acting together, they will not be subordinate to the 'I' attitude of any particular person or group of persons, but will always be shaping themselves as a 'we'. Peaceful coexistence in a society of strangers is achieved not by a common purpose or a regimented plan, but by side-constraints, which protect each person from the purposes and plans of everyone else. The same is true in the affairs of nations, which coexist peacefully when they obey the constraints of international law. Peaceful coexistence is not, however, secured by a common purpose or a comprehensive plan, and if peace exists in Europe today it is not because of the plan but in spite of it.

This point was noticed, though in quite other terms, by Burke when he attacked the thinking behind the French Revolution. The Revolutionaries, Burke argued, were guided by an 'armed doctrine', which they put forward as justifying their destructive actions. Everything was subordinate to the great plan, of establishing a society of 'liberty, equality and fraternity' – goals whose very vagueness served to conceal the deep contradiction hidden within them. If people have liberty, then they will use it in ways that lead of their own accord to inequality. If people are to be equal, then their liberty must be removed. In the event the Revolutionaries abolished liberty, and established on its ruin a new form of inequality – between those with political power, who were the masters, and those without it, who were the slaves. This result was the inevitable consequence, in Burke's view, of the revolutionary emphasis on Reason – the rational pursuit of an overarching plan. In place of Reason, so understood, Burke advocated tradition, by which he meant the kind of reasonableness enshrined in long-term solutions, which had arisen by trial, error and consensus over time, and through the free cooperation of individuals. The 'reason' of the Revolutionaries was the voice of a collective 'I' against the 'we' of tradition.

Tradition is not part of a plan of action, but arises from the enterprise of social cooperation over time. And it arises from the application of moral constraints of the kind enshrined in the 'natural law' – constraints within which the cooperation of strangers to their mutual advantage becomes possible. As with the market the benefit that these constraints confer is in part epistemic: they provide knowledge that has stood the test of time, by permitting the resolution of conflicts and the re-establishment of social equilibrium in the face of local disturbances. By following traditional rules and customs we equip ourselves with practical knowledge that will be especially useful when venturing forth into the unforeseeable – namely knowledge of how to conduct ourselves towards others, so as to secure their cooperation in advancing our aims.

To put the point in another way, tradition (and the common law as a fundamental application of it) condenses into itself the fruits of a long history of human experience: it provides knowledge that can be neither contained in a formula nor confined to a single human head, but which is dispersed across time, in the historical experience of an evolving community. Just as prices in a market condense into themselves information that is otherwise dispersed throughout contemporary society, so do laws condense information that is dispersed over a society's past. To put Burke's point in a modern idiom somewhat removed from his own majestic periods: the knowledge that we need in the unforeseeable circumstances of human life is neither derived from nor contained in the experience of a single person, nor can it be deduced *a priori* from universal laws. This knowledge is bequeathed to us by customs, institutions and habits of thought that have shaped themselves over generations, through the trials and errors of people many of whom have perished in the course of acquiring it.

And this returns me, in conclusion, to the Austrian theory of the market in the version advanced by Hayek. Implicit in Hayek is the thought that free exchange and enduring customs are to be justified in exactly the same terms. Both are indispensable distillations of socially necessary knowledge, the one operating synchronously, the other diachronically, in order to bring the experiences of indefinitely many others to bear on the decision taken by me, here, now. Hayek emphasizes the free market as part of a wider spontaneous order founded in the free exchange of goods, ideas and interests – the 'game of catallaxy' as he calls it. But this game is played over time, and – to adapt a thought of Burke's – the dead and the unborn are also players, who make their presence known through traditions, institutions and laws. Those who believe that social order demands constraints on the market are right. But in a true spontaneous order the constraints are already there, in the form of customs, laws and morals. If those good things decay, then there is no way, according to Hayek, that legislation can replace them. For they arise spontaneously or not at all, and the imposition of legislative edicts for the 'good society' destroys what remains of the accumulated wisdom that makes such a society possible. It is not surprising therefore if British conservative thinkers – notably Hume, Smith, Burke and Oakeshott – have tended to see no tension between a defence of the free market and a traditionalist vision of social order. For they have put their faith in the spontaneous limits placed on the market by the moral consensus of the community. Maybe that consensus is now breaking down. But the breakdown is in part the result of state interference, and certainly unlikely to be cured by it. It is precisely the success of the planning fallacy in erecting vast engines of power and influence, careering out of control into the future, that has led to the erosion of the consensus that places a genuine 'we' in the centre of politics.

SEVEN

The Moving Spirit Fallacy

Earlier I praised Hegel for his recognition that freedom is not a natural gift but an artefact that we construct together through our shared social membership. But Hegel bequeathed to the world – without altogether intending to do so – a way of thinking that is as fallacious as any of those that he attacked, and which has had a profound influence on the incautious enthusiasms that have turned our world upside down in the last century. This way of thinking holds that history exhibits a continuous development, and that this development parallels the spiritual development of the individual towards full self-consciousness, and also the development of society towards its realization in the law-governed and objective state. Each successive period of history, according to the Hegelians, exhibits a stage in the spiritual development of mankind – a particular 'spirit of the time' or *Zeitgeist*, which is the common property of all contemporary cultural products, and which is inherently dynamic, transforming what it inherits and being superseded when its time is over.

Hegel's philosophy of history was an attempt to make sense of a striking but mysterious phenomenon, which is the forward movement of Western societies, and the gradual emergence of the free individual as the focus and *raison d'être* of the modern state.[55] Much of what he wrote was wild speculation, but much more was real insight and measured explanation. The problem lies with the concept of the *Zeitgeist*, which in Hegel is connected with a subtle theory of temporal processes and the 'objectification' (*Entäusserung*) of the collective spirit. In the hands of less subtle thinkers this idea of the 'spirit of the time' was vulgarized into a rhetorical weapon with which to justify innovation in every sphere, and to rationalize a wholesale repudiation of the past. It is the root conception in the philosophy of progress, and has had an impact on the political and intellectual life of the modern world quite out of proportion to its plausibility. And it gives rise to an interesting fallacy, the workings of which are everywhere to be observed in the cultural and political life of modern societies.

I call this fallacy the 'moving spirit' fallacy: the fallacy of assimilating all that is happening in the world that you inhabit, your own projects included, to the 'spirit of the times'. You commit the moving spirit fallacy every time you see the free actions of living individuals as the necessary consequences of the

---

55 Hegel, *Lectures on the Philosophy of History*, trans. H. B. Nisbet, Cambridge, 1980.

times in which they live. This is a fallacy not only because it denies human freedom. It is a fallacy for two further reasons. First, because it applies a method for making sense of the past to the present and the future. Secondly, because it applies an understanding of progress derived from science to the generality of human culture.

The moving spirit fallacy, in its common forms, bears the imprint of Hegelian art history. In the wake of Hegel's philosophy of history and his posthumous lectures on aesthetics there emerged an influential movement in German-speaking universities devoted to the periodization of Western culture. Great thinkers like Jakob Burckhardt and his pupil Heinrich Wölfflin attempted to understand European civilization in terms of successive movements in the world of ideas, each of which imposed a certain unity of outlook and inspiration on the art and literature of its time. This was how Wölfflin tried to make sense of the art and architecture of seventeenth-century Europe, which saw a rapid transformation of the classical grammar and solid, earthbound forms of the Renaissance to the dancing, heaven-directed churches of Borromini, to the gesticulating sculptures of Bernini and the dark dramatic tableaux of Rubens and Caravaggio. It seemed to Wölfflin that the very same transition from civic forms to personal dramas could be witnessed in the painting, the sculpture and the architecture of the mid-seventeenth century, and that it could be witnessed not only in Italy but in France and Germany too. Just as Burckhardt had justified the idea of the Renaissance by showing how it displayed itself in all the arts and sciences of fifteenth-century Italy, so did Wölfflin propose to justify the idea of the Baroque, by a similar synthesis of all the relevant spheres of cultural expression.[56]

Thus was invented the category of the Baroque, which – for all its broadness and generality – has served a valuable purpose in enabling us, who look back on all this from our vantage point, knowing what came later as well as what came before, to make sense of it as a totality. Wölfflin connected the Baroque with the Counter-Reformation in religion, and with the great political and religious conflicts that were fragmenting contemporary Europe. And he was consciously influenced in this by the philosophy of Hegel, believing that civilization moves forward from period to period in its entirety, as an organism passes from one stage of development to the next in its life-cycle. So influential was this method of periodization that the term 'Baroque' is now applied to everything that happened in the world of European culture during the seventeenth and early eighteenth centuries, so that, for example, Milton is described as a Baroque poet. Indeed, the category of the Baroque has become established in musicology as a convenient label with which to bring Vivaldi, Bach and Couperin together, as successors to Renaissance polyphony and precursors of the 'classical style' – a style that was also, for a while, called Rococo, on the understanding that in music, as in architecture,

56   Jakob Burckhardt, *The Civilization of the Renaissance in Italy*, 1860; Heinrich Wölfflin, *Renaissance and Baroque*, 1888.

Rococo succeeds Baroque with the inexorable logic with which one collective *Zeitgeist* follows another.

It is very clear that this way of thinking about art and culture is both helpful, in emphasizing the connections and unities among art-forms, and also prodigal of forced connections. It is clear too that it is essentially a *retrospective* form of thought. It depends upon a vantage point from which the landscape of the past can be seen as shaped by heights, depths and boundaries, whose shadows and continuities are visible only from a sufficient distance. It involves arranging diverse and often conflicting appearances according to current interests that would have been incomprehensible to people of those distant times; and it presupposes a long-term historical perspective that is available only to those who identify themselves as 'later than' the thing they study. To suppose that you can look at your own times in this frame of mind, that you can explore 'what the *Zeitgeist* now requires', and even project that exploration forwards into an unknowable future, is to commit a dangerous fallacy – dangerous because it involves limiting your freedom and seeing what is wholly accidental under the aspect of necessity.

To put the point slightly differently: periodization of the kind familiar in the history of art is not the first step towards a scientific theory. It is not aiming to produce universal 'laws of motion' to which all human cultures must conform – even though Hegel believed that such laws could be discovered. It is an exercise in what the Kantian philosopher Wilhelm Dilthey called *Verstehen*, and which we might call 'humane understanding', the kind of understanding that we direct towards each other through reason-giving dialogue. It is a kind of understanding that respects the freedom of its object. However, because it is directed towards the past, and by way of making sense of its *historical* character, its findings have an air of ineluctability. After all, the past is over and done with; it is not to be changed. And by fast-forwarding to the present, while still keeping our historian's spectacles fixed to our head, we are coaxed into thinking exactly the same of *now* – that everything we do, we do ineluctably, in obedience to the moving spirit that carries us all along.

The fallacy is aggravated by the myth of 'progress'. In the sphere of scientific advance it is undeniable that there is progress: that is to say, each generation builds on the knowledge acquired by its predecessor, and one by one the secrets of the universe are unlocked and exploited. Of course, there is no reason why this process should go on forever, and it is quite conceivable that one day educational institutions will decline to such a point that the accumulated results of scientific investigation will no longer be passed on. But failing such an eventuality, it lies in the nature of the case that science makes progress, and that this progress trans-lates into technological achievements that in turn influence the social condition and expectations of people.

On the other hand, it is clearly fallacious to think that this kind of progress is exhibited in spheres where there is no underlying accumulation of knowledge on which to build. It is inherently questionable to believe, for example, that there is continuous *moral* progress, moving forward with the speed of science; still more questionable to believe that there is artistic or spiritual progress marching beside it. Virtually no poet since Homer has surpassed him, and in the arts, in religious thought and in philosophical speculation, we are as likely to encounter a decline from one generation to the next as an improvement. Even if there is knowledge of a sort contained in a high culture, it is not knowledge of the kind that accumulates in an orderly or linear way. It is a matter of wisdom, not expertise, of an imaginative grasp of the human condition rather than the search for theories with which to explain it.

There is one place, however, where the belief in progress leaks into territory that it poisons, and that is politics. Political, legal and administrative institutions are constantly changing in response to the interests and arguments of those subject to them. And in certain places and times the change has seemed progressive – advancing the cause of emancipation step by step, as monarchical and ecclesiastical powers are steadily driven into retreat before the tide of popular sovereignty. That is a story told in many ways, and it is not my purpose in this book to take issue with it, but only to point out that, while there are many aspects of political order that admit of progressive change, not all change is positive, and none of it occurs without intricate management and the balance of competing interests. The political emancipation of the ordinary subject, and the transition from subject to citizen, certainly occurred in eighteenth-century America. It was announced by the French Revolution, but also thwarted by it. And the progress made everywhere in the nineteenth century came to an abrupt end in Russia in 1917, in Germany twenty years later, and in Eastern Europe after the Second World War. At no point could it be said that this process of emancipation was *inevitable*, that it was driven by the inexorable changes of the *Zeitgeist*, or that it had the kind of dialectical logic – the logic of successive question and answer – that a Hegelian would see in it. There are those like Francis Fukuyama who see a continuous advance since the Enlightenment from relations of power and subordination to a final equality of respect, which will mark 'the end of history'.[57] But the thesis looks plausible only if we focus on a narrow range of examples, and only if we ignore the many ways in which this equality of respect has been achieved by making respect entirely obsolete.

Let us at least say that progress in the political sphere is both uncertain and disputed. Change occurs – sometimes from worse to better, sometimes from better to worse. But it is only in retrospect, in the light cast by cultural and social history, that we can speak of a *Zeitgeist* that involved just *this* or *that* by way of change or development. At a certain moment, however, some time towards the middle of the nineteenth century, when the idea of progress was enthroned in politics, and when scientific discovery was both overthrowing established beliefs and vastly augmenting

57   Francis Fukuyama, *The End of History and the Last Man*, Harmondsworth, 1992.

human competence, the idea became current that we had entered a new era – the era of modernity. This was the moment when the moving spirit fallacy began to proliferate. In every sphere it was held that we must be true to the spirit of the times, that to adhere to old customs, old values, old practices, whether in politics, in social relations or in artistic expression, was simply 'reactionary', a failure to understand the laws of historical development, and a refusal of the 'new dawn' that was breaking before our eyes. This was the message broadcast in the moral and political sphere by the British Utilitarians, the French Positivists and Saint-Simonians, and the Young Hegelians in Germany. It could fairly be said that the belief in a moving spirit on which mankind was being carried forward to ever-increasing knowledge, competence and mastery over nature, became, during the nineteenth century, a reigning superstition, and one that had a particularly devastating effect in Russia, as Dostoevsky and others observed. And the superstition has survived into our times, in the panaceas of the utopians, in the reckless rhetoric of the globalizers, and in the unscrupulous futurism of the transhumanists.

The fallacy here, of taking a retrospective view of something that has not yet happened, became an integral part of progressive thinking not only in politics but also in the arts. The result is a paradox – a belief in historical forces that free us, but through laws that bind us. This paradox is familiar from Lenin and Mao, who constantly exhort us to do freely what they believe us to be bound to do in any case. Equally familiar is the destruction that

results when people imagine themselves to be excused by historical 'laws of motion' that they can do nothing to avert. More
interesting for us today, however, is the effect of this fallacy on
the practice of art and architecture.

For over a century it has been orthodoxy that works of art and
architecture should be new departures: not just original but also
in some way challenging, even shocking, in their defiance of the
expectations of those who come across them. That the critics were
wrong to be dismissive of Manet, equally wrong to be scornful of
abstract art, goes without saying. But those episodes should be
seen as aberrations. For the most part new and original works of
art receive the just appreciation of the critical public – think of the
crowds at Beethoven's funeral, or the reception of T. S. Eliot,
Henry Moore and Picasso. It is by no means normal for an artist
to achieve success by shocking, outraging or challenging his
audience. Nor has originality been conceived, in previous ages,
as a radical overthrow of all previous conventions, or a completely new departure and a transgression of aesthetic norms.
Michelangelo, in his interior to the Laurentian Library in
Florence, defied the syntax of classical architecture – but in ways
that were interesting and intelligible to those accustomed to the
Brunelleschian style, and while using the classical vocabulary and
proportions as his raw material. The result was startling to his
contemporaries, but also immediately popular. Mozart, by
contrast, adopted in his string quartets the idiom perfected by
Haydn, and hardly strayed from it. Yet, as Haydn himself

acknowledged, they are among the most original works of music ever composed.

Nonetheless, it has become a commonplace to defend every new departure in the world of art, music and architecture, however empty or offensive, with a platitudinous reference to the 'resistance' supposedly encountered by great artists in any period. Gilbert and George's empty collages, Tracey Emin's unmade bed, Damien Hirst's sharks in formaldehyde are all praised as original experiments that deserve the highest accolades. No critic would dare to suggest that they might be as meaningless as they appear, for fear of being lumped with those who excluded Manet from the Salon, or who booed at the *Rite of Spring*. We are all familiar with the rhetoric here, and the ease with which offensive gestures are rebranded as original ideas, in order to conform to the standard forms of aesthetic praise.

Behind all this, it seems to me, lies the moving spirit fallacy. It tells us that the attempt to adhere to standards and rules established in previous generations is essentially reactionary, an exercise in 'nostalgia' or 'pastiche'. There is no going back, since it is impossible to *belong* to another time, only to imitate it in ways that will inevitably be slavish, inauthentic and insincere. The *Zeitgeist* that governs us is the one in action *now*. Real art must be true to the *Zeitgeist*; and if it shocks, that is only because the future is bound to shock those who are not prepared for it, and who do not recognize its necessity. The paradox, that the freedom and transgression of the truly modern artist are the products of an ineluctable law, is unhesitatingly embraced by the orthodoxy. Truly modern artists belong to their time, and it is the time that dictates what they do.

From that fallacious way of thinking much trivial art has flowed. But so too has great art, which always transcends the critical orthodoxies used to justify it, so as to establish itself with an authority that is above theory, and above apologetics. The *Zeitgeist* fallacy was used to justify the music of Berg, Webern and Schoenberg, and the fallaciousness of the justification in no way counts against the validity of the cause. What is objectionable is the use of the fallacy in the manner of Adorno, to create a critical orthodoxy that prevents all experiments other than those permitted by the reigning spirit, which therefore cease to be experiments at all and become the ineluctable voice of history.[58] That orthodoxy makes real criticism redundant. Moreover it gives rise to a pernicious substitute for criticism. If a work is difficult, outrageous, shocking or sacrilegious then it should be praised; if it is guided by the old rules and decencies then it should be dismissed. That simple rule makes it easy for critics to exercise their profession, and to make mistakes, if at all, only through being too much on the side of the future. It makes art and composition easy, and enables incompetent pretenders to dismiss the hard-won beauties of their contemporaries as mere pastiche – as Adorno dismissed Sibelius, Vaughan Williams and, in the end, even Stravinsky, as purveyors of the musical 'fetish'.

58   See Theodor W. Adorno, *The Philosophy of Modern Music*, tr. Anne G. Mitchell and Wesley V. Blomster, London, 2003 (first published in 1948).

A dose of pessimism reminds us that great art is not easy to come by, that there is no formula for producing it, and that creativity makes sense only if there are also the rules that constrain it. Those rules are not arbitrary or invented. Like the syntax of tonal harmony they have evolved through the dialogue over centuries between artist and public. They are the by-products of taste, the residues of successful communication, to follow which is to gain access to a continuous tradition of enjoyment. The rules can be broken, but they must first be internalized. We respect Schoenberg's breaking the rules in *Pierrot Lunaire*, partly because they were being broken by the composer of *Gurrelieder* and *Verklärte Nacht*. We don't respect the random breaking of rules by someone, such as Tracey Emin, who seems never to have mastered them.

As for the moving spirit fallacy, it owes its appeal to its vacuity: it can be used to justify anything, to override all criticism, however well informed, and to greet with empty accolades whatever facetious act of defiance can present itself as new. It endows the most arbitrary of gestures with a specious aura of necessity, and so neutralizes criticism before it has been voiced. And it damages both the cause of tradition (against which it is levelled) and the cause of individual talent (which it purports to advance). From Schoenberg and Eliot to Messiaen and Matisse, the great modernists have had no time for a view that makes modern art easy and neglects the important feature without which originality is imperceivable, which is the attempt to establish real continuity with the masters of the past. The early modernists, while to some extent infected with the *Zeitgeist* fallacy, nevertheless felt that their freedom had to be *justified*, and that it could be justified only by *belonging* with the past, and not by ignoring it or defying it. The true history of the modern artist is the story told by the great modernists themselves. It is the story told by T. S. Eliot in his essays and the *Four Quartets*, by Ezra Pound in the *Cantos*, by Schoenberg in his critical writings and in *Moses und Aron*, by Rilke in the *Sonnets to Orpheus* and by Valéry in *Le cimetière marin*. And it sees the goal of the modern artist not as a break with tradition, but as a recapturing of tradition, in circumstances for which the artistic legacy has made little or no provision. This story does not see the pastness of the present moment but its present reality, as *the place we have got to*, and whose nature must be understood in terms of a continuum. If, in modern circumstances, the forms and styles of art must be remade, this is not in order to repudiate the old tradition, but in order to restore it. The effort of the modern artist is to express realities that have not been encountered before and which are especially hard to encompass. But this cannot be done except by bringing the spiritual capital of our culture to bear on the present moment and to show it as it truly is. For Eliot and his colleagues, therefore, there could be no truly modern art that was not at the same time a search for orthodoxy: an attempt to capture the nature of the modern experience by setting it in relation to the certainties of a real tradition.

The most telling illustration of the moving spirit fallacy is that presented by modern architecture and its apologists. By 'modern architecture' I do not mean the masterworks that, from Frank Lloyd Wright to Louis Kahn, have taken their place among the icons of our times. I mean the modern vernacular, composed of curtain walls or horizontal slabs, without mouldings, shadows or ornaments, without articulate façades, standing as a familiar adversary in our streets, towns and countryside – the familiar 'shoe box' style that you can find on the edge, and increasingly in the centre, of our towns. The apologists for this kind of everyday modernism dominate our schools of architecture. They reject the classical Orders, columns, architraves and mouldings. They reject the Greek and the Gothic revivals. They reject the street as the primary public space and the façade as the public aspect of a building. They reject every written and unwritten rule that once shaped the urban fabric. They reject these things as residues of 'another time', which can be imitated now only from a condition of 'inauthenticity', and only by engaging in what the modernists call 'pastiche'. History has decreed an end to such things; a new dawn has broken, and with it a new architecture, with materials and methods that belong to the spirit of the times.

The leading theorists of modernism – Le Corbusier, the Russian constructivists, Walter Gropius and Hannes Meyer – claimed to be architectural thinkers in the tradition of Vitruvius and Palladio. However, the paltriness of what they said about architecture (compared with what had been said by the revivalists – for example, by Alberti in his *Ten Books on Architecture*, by

Ruskin in *Stones of Venice* and *The Seven Lamps of Architecture* and by Viollet-le-Duc in his two volumes of lectures) reveals this claim to be a sham. The modernist pioneers were social and political activists, who wished to squeeze the disorderly human material that constitutes a city into a utopian straitjacket. Architecture for them was one part of a new and all-comprehending plan. Le Corbusier's project to demolish all of Paris north of the Seine and replace it with high-rise towers of glass was supposed to be an emancipation, a liberation from the old constraints of urban living. Those dirty, promiscuous streets and alleyways were to be replaced with grass and trees – open spaces where the new human type, released from the hygienic glass bottle where he was stored by night, could walk in the sunshine and be alone with himself. The fact is, however, that Le Corbusier never asked himself whether people wanted to live in this utopia, nor did he care what method was used to transport them there. History (as understood by the modernist project) required them to be there, and that was that.

That way of thinking displays many of the fallacies already discussed in this work. The best case fallacy has had a particularly powerful input into architectural thinking from the first days of the Bauhaus, whose occupants showed a marked refusal to look at the worst that might result from their stupendous housing projects. The accumulated wisdom of builders and planners down the centuries was set aside purely on the strength of a 'best case' vision of the new ways of living. Light, air and verdure would replace the dingy street and the stinking alleyway. As for darkness, intimacy, street life and thresholds, nobody bothered to consult the mere human beings who had shown, over generations, their love and need for those things.

It is not only Europe and America that has suffered the implacable march of the architectural modernists. When Mohamed Atta flew American Airlines Flight 11 into the north tower of the World Trade Center on 11 September 2001 he was certainly expressing his resentment towards everything symbolized by that building: the triumph of secular materialism, the success and prosperity of America, the tyranny of high finance and the hubris of the modern city. But he was also expressing a long-standing grudge against architectural modernism, which he had already voiced in his Master's dissertation for the University of Hamburg architecture school. The theme of that dissertation was the old city of Aleppo, damaged by Syrian President Hafez al-Assad in his merciless war of extermination against the Muslim Brotherhood, but damaged far more by the jerry-built skyscrapers that cancel the lines of the ancient streets, and rise high above the slim imploring fingers of the mosques. This junkyard modernism was, for Atta, a symbol of the impiety of the modern world, and of its brutal disregard towards the Muslim city.

The old cities of the Middle East, recorded in Edward Lear's delightful drawings and watercolours, were places where tightly knit communities huddled in the shadows of the mosques, and minarets punctured the sky in a constant attitude of prayer. They were places of pious industry, and their romantic alleyways, courtyards and bazaars – the familiar background to Arab story-telling from the *Thousand and One Nights* to the novels of Naguib Mahfouz – have an immovable place in the longings of Muslims, especially those, like Atta, who find themselves drifting among strangers in the concrete wastes of a modern Western city.

Those old cities of the Middle East are very different today, with mosques squeezed pathetically between giant skyscrapers, poorly built apartment blocks squashing the old courtyards, and alleyways torn asunder by highways. And, although the causes of this social and aesthetic disaster are many, overpopulation being one of them, it is undeniable that architectural modernism must take some part of the blame. For it feeds directly into that desire to 'move forward with the times' that is the only alternative in the mind of the Middle Eastern bureaucrat to the inward-looking submission that has hitherto been the norm. It was Le Corbusier's insane plan for Algiers that first suggested that the old Muslim cities could be entirely refashioned in total disregard of the social and spiritual needs of their residents, so as to belong at last to the modern world. Although only one section of the plan was ever built, the plan itself is nevertheless studied assiduously in schools of architecture as one of the great 'solutions' to a problem that, prior to Le Corbusier, had never existed – the 'problem' of pack-ing people into a city while allowing free movement across it, so as to create a city that would be a symbol of the new age of the motor car. Le Corbusier's solution was to put highways in the air, with the people shovelled into apartment blocks beneath them. Ancient homes and corridor streets were to be demolished, and huge tower blocks were to front the ocean, dwarfing mosques and churches. The plans were opposed by the elected mayor of the city, which led Le Corbusier to approach the unelected governor of the *Département*, asking him to overrule the mayor. 'The plan must rule,' he wrote. 'It is the plan which is right. It proclaims indubitable realities.' And when he led the Vichy Government's commission on national building in 1941, Le Corbusier insisted on putting his plans for Algiers at the top of the agenda.[59]

The congested nature of the Muslim city is the natural by-product of a way of life. Courtyards and alleyways express the very soul of this community – a community that stops to pray five times a day, that defines itself through obedience and submission, and retreats into the family whenever the going gets tough. Highways and tower blocks are precisely the things that kill the Muslim city and send its children abroad, raging like Atta for revenge against the modernist attitudes that have uprooted them. Yet the *Zeitgeist* demanded that such cities be destroyed, and they had no defence against it. Nor were the Muslim countries innocent of the moving spirit fallacy. On the contrary, the most depressing thing about them has been their rush to adopt the symbols of modernity, and to define modernity in terms of the changes that have made American cities into uninhabitable

---

59   The story is told by John Silber, *Architecture of the Absurd*, Boston, 2007.

deserts. It was not a rational assessment of Egypt's energy needs that led to the building of the Aswan Dam, and the drowning of a beautiful area rich in antiquities. It was the very same historicist superstitition that had led to Pevsner's dismissal of Victorian Gothic, to Le Corbusier's rage against old Algiers, and to the building in London of the absurd Millennium Dome. Indeed, if we are seeking an explanation of Islamism this is the place to begin, in the official adoption by the new bureaucrats of a fallacy that denies legitimacy to a faith and a way of life that are intrinsically backward-looking. Islam, properly conceived, does not accept either that we can move with the times or that there *are* such things as 'times' with which we might 'move'. Written everywhere over the face of the Islamic world is a painful conflict, between modernist bureaucracies shaped by the moving spirit fallacy, and communities for whom the ruling spirit is eternal, immovable, all-knowing and outside time and change. And when Muslims become Islamists, it is in part because they have adopted the fallacy of their bureaucratic opponents, so as to perceive the world and its history as a manifestation of a rival moving spirit.

Classical and Gothic buildings speak of another age, in which faith, honour and authority stood proudly and without self-mockery in the street. For the modernists, their styles and materials could no longer be used sincerely, since nobody believed in those old ideals. The modern age was an age without heroes, without faith, without public tribute to anything higher or more dignified than the common man. It needed an architecture that would reflect its moral vision, of a classless society from which all hierarchies had disappeared, a society with no absolute, but only relative values. Hence it needed an architecture without ornament and without any other pretence to a grandeur beyond the reach of mortal beings, an architecture that used modern materials to create a modern world. The key words of this new architecture were 'honesty' and 'function'. By being honest, it was implied, buildings could help *us* to become so. The new city of glass, concrete and parkland would be a city without social pretence, where people would live in exemplary uniformity and be rewarded with equal respect. It is the city that the *Zeitgeist* demands.

Paradoxically, however, the architect who was to create the new anti-heroic city would himself become the hero. There emerged with the modernists a vision of the architect as Titan, manipulating vast structures and extended spaces. The architect was to replace the petty order of the street and alleyway – the order of the invisible hand – with a new, planned and compre-hended order, a monument to the visible hand that was creating it. This vision of the architect is already there in Ibsen's *The Master-Builder*, and was made popular by the novelist and philosopher Ayn Rand in her striking book *Atlas Shrugged*. The modernist city began as a city without monuments, and it became a monument in itself – a monument to its architect. And no reader of Le Corbusier can fail to see the marks of this egomaniacal conception in everything he wrote. The very same egomania is visible in the forms and scales adopted by the 'starchitects', such as Richard Rogers and Norman Foster, who have been let loose on our cities. And it is the principal reason why many people recoil from their buildings: there, before us, is the 'I' attitude, crying in triumph from the midst of a mutilated 'we'.

One of the most remarkable characteristics of the modern movement in architecture has been the venom with which it cleared a space for itself. Those opposed to it were regarded as enemies, reactionaries, nostalgists, who were impeding the necessary march of history. They were to be removed as soon as possible from positions of influence and power. When the German art historian Nikolaus Pevsner and the Russian constructivist architect Berthold Lubetkin brought the crusade to London they set up shop as legislators, condemning everything that was not conceived as a radical break with the past. Both were travelling as refugees from modernism of the political variety – Nazism in Pevsner's case, communism in Lubetkin's. But they brought with them the censorious attitudes of the regimes from which they fled. Nothing was more loathsome in their eyes than the would-be enchantment of a neo-classical school or a Victorian Gothic bank. To Pevsner, Arthur Street's great Gothic law courts, which are the centrepiece of London's legal quarter and a fitting symbol of common law justice and its daily work of reconciliation, were mediocre buildings of no consequence, whose fairytale pinnacles and marble columns were neither uplifting nor cheerful but merely pretence. By contrast the underground station at

Arnos Grove, with its plain wrapped brickwork and its grim metal-frame windows, was a portent of a future and better world in which modern life would be honestly portrayed and openly accepted.

In the face of this ideological onslaught, conducted with all the apparatus of German scholarship, and with a mesmerizing trust in the future and the new man who was to arise in it, people lost hold of their saving pessimism. And in doing so, they neglected to examine the motives of the modernists and their supporters. They forgot that there is a vast amount of money to be made by demolishing ancient streets and putting tower blocks in their stead, and that this money had not been made by architects in the past for the same reason that ordinary women had not become rich from prostitution, or ordinary businessmen from smuggling – namely, that culture and morality had stood in the way. There is a powerful vested interest in the view that aesthetic standards must always be changing in obedience to the *Zeitgeist*.

Subtract the profit-makers and the vandals, however, and ask ordinary people how their town should be designed – not for their private good, but for the common good – and a surprising level of agreement will be reached, as has been exemplified down the ages. People have agreed, for example, on scale: nothing too big for the residential quarters, nothing too broad or tall or domineering for the public parts. They have agreed on the need for streets, and for doors and windows opening on to the streets. They have agreed that buildings should follow the contours of streets, and not slice across them or in any way arrogate to themselves spaces that are recognizably public and permeable. They have agreed that lighting should be low, discreet and if possible mounted on permanent structures. They have agreed on the humanity of some materials and the alienating quality of others; they have even agreed about details such as mouldings, window-frames and paving stones, as soon as they have learned to think of them as chosen not for their personal benefit, but for the common good. The classical style in architecture, and in particular the pattern-book vernacular familiar from old Manhattan and Georgian London, embodies this kind of reflective agreement. The principles that guide it are obeyed equally in the streets of ancient Ephesus and in the precincts of our Gothic abbeys and cathedrals.

At a certain point Prince Charles took advantage of his public position to voice those thoughts, speaking on behalf of the silent majority. And the outrage of the architectural establishment was expressed in familiar terms. The Prince has been described as 'living in another century', as 'reactionary', as unable to understand that 'the world has moved on', as 'out of touch' with the genuine and 'original' work of people 'living and working now'. His own attempts, through the architect Léon Krier, to construct a model new town at Poundbury in Dorset are dismissed as 'Disneyland', 'pastiche', 'twee' and 'backward-looking'. All those epithets, which you can find at every point in the discussions that have followed the Prince's famous, indeed notorious speech against the modernist 'carbuncles' that disfigure London,[60] show the moving spirit fallacy at work, and the way in which it is used to close discussion of what should be an open question – the question of how you and I should build, here and now.

Heidegger, not otherwise given to lucid utterance, made an important contribution in arguing that 'we attain to dwelling... only by means of building'.[61] He could have put the point the other way round with equal truth: only by learning how to build do we attain to dwelling. Building and dwelling are two parts of a single action. Architecture is the art of settlement. From this simple observation we can understand at once how destructive the moving spirit fallacy must be when imported from the realm of art-historical scholarship, in order to set itself up as a guide to the present. It is the inevitable enemy of urban design, and has proved itself to be so. And so it is hardly surprising if our cities, subjected to the rule of this fallacy, should have fallen so completely apart. A jumble of mutually antagonistic 'I's has replaced the old consensus of the city, and the 'we' of common settlement, once expressed in alleyway, doorway, architrave, façade and street, has retreated from view.

60 Speech delivered at the 150th anniversary of the Royal Institute of British Architects, 30 May 1984.

61 See Martin Heidegger, 'Building, Dwelling, Thinking', in *Poetry, Language, Thought*, tr. Alfred Hofstadter, New York, 1971; Eduard Führ, *Bauen und Wohnen: Martin Heideggers Grundlegung einer Phänomenologie der Architektur*, Münster and New York, 2000.

EIGHT

The Aggregation Fallacy

When the French Revolutionaries crafted their famous slogan, *Liberté, égalité, fraternité*, they were in a state of utopian exaltation that prevented them from seeing any fault in it. In their eyes liberty was good, equality was good and fraternity was good, so the combination was thrice good. That is like saying lobster is good, chocolate is good, ketchup is good, so lobster cooked in chocolate and ketchup is thrice good. Of course, American cooking exemplifies that kind of mistake in ways that never cease to appal the discerning European palate. But in the political sphere mistakes have consequences far worse than any to be found on an American plate.

The French had to go through a painful process of discovery before realizing what they had embarked on. Even when Robespierre fanatically promoted 'the despotism of liberty' it did not dawn on the Jacobins that they were committed to a contradiction. Only with the Revolutionary tribunals – in which judge, jury and prosecutor were identical and the accused deprived of the right of defence – did the more sensible among them see that the goal of equality requires the destruction of liberty. And the heads in which that thought began to germinate were quickly cut off before it could bring forth fruit. Again and again since those days, however, humanity has made the same mistake, dressing up the pursuit of equality as the *true* form of liberty, and advocating enslavement by the state as the 'liberation' of the masses from the bonds of exploitation.

The thinking here embodies a fallacy that is replicated whenever the desire for good things impetuously cancels any attempt to understand the connections between them. As people aspire to one good thing after another, they project their hope away from themselves, imagining it to be realized in some future human condition. As a result they add one good to another in an ever-expanding wish-list. And because each good has been taken from its context and transferred to an imaginary world, the result is almost certain to involve aims that cannot be advanced together.

This – the 'aggregation' fallacy – has played a major part in the evolution of liberalism, from its classical form, espoused by Adam Smith, to its modern form in the worldview of American East Coast intellectuals, and enshrined in John Rawls's magisterial *A Theory of Justice*. For our Victorian ancestors a liberal was someone who valued individual freedom more highly than any social goal that could be imposed by the state, and who believed that individuals would solve their problems through their innate moral sense, provided only that the state allowed them to exercise it. In America today a liberal is someone who advocates massive interference by the state in all economic activity, in schools and universities, in the institutions of civil society such as marriage and associations, in order to impose equality.

The history of American liberalism has raised the question whether liberty and equality really can be combined in the way that so many people have wished. Is the conflict between them negotiable? It is to the credit of Rawls that he looked for an answer to that question, and thought that he had found it in the ingenious idea of a 'lexical ordering'. The requirement of liberty must be satisfied before questions of distribution can be raised. However, the requirement of liberty is one of *equal* liberty, and this raises the problem all over again. What if we can make liberty equal only by removing it?

We see the force of this question in political practice. Assaults on the liberties hitherto enjoyed by Americans are carried out, as a rule, in the name of liberty. For example, when an employer's liberty to employ whom he wishes is cancelled by 'non-discrimination' policies, this is justified as 'empowering' and therefore 'liberating' previously oppressed minorities. If it is argued that the rights of the employer are infringed by policies that compel him to do what he would not do voluntarily, then the Supreme Court discovers rights of the employee that will override those rights. These new rights of the employee are not like the individual rights enshrined in the original Bill of Rights, which are really freedoms, defining the sphere of individual sovereignty. They are group rights – rights that a person has by virtue of being a woman, a homosexual, a member of a minority, or whatever. This can be seen in disputes over 'affirmative action'. Two people, John and Mary, apply for admission to a college. John has better qualifications, but Mary is a native American and is admitted on that ground. In such cases liberals argue that Mary has a right to the advantage bestowed on her by virtue of the group to which she belongs – a previously oppressed group whose position in society can be remedied only by such preferential treatment.

This new kind of right is invented in order to justify discrimination in the name of non-discrimination. It is a way of cancelling individual rights in the interest of groups. As such it runs counter to the whole meaning of liberalism in its classical form, which aimed to protect the individual against the group, and to guarantee the individual's sovereignty over his own life, as the sole basis for a consensual order. Yet American liberals have no doubt in their own minds that it is they, and not their conservative opponents, who are the true advocates of individual freedom in the modern world. The desire for equality is, in their eyes, nothing less than the desire to make freedom equally available – something that can be achieved only by 'empowering' the groups whose disadvantages have hitherto prevented them from pursuing their aims. And the only agent capable of this large-scale act of empowerment is the state, which must be expanded accordingly.

It is not my concern to take sides in this conflict. I suspect that most people will be pulled both ways, recognizing the dubious nature of 'group rights', while still hoping that the adverse position of previously oppressed minorities can be improved by legal and constitutional procedures. Nevertheless, the conflict illustrates the way in which liberty and equality are at war, as well as the way in which people take sides in the war without admitting its existence. 'Liberal' judges will interpret the US Constitution in whatever way is needed to generate equality, and they will justify this by saying that they are discerning hitherto unnoticed *rights*. Hence regulation of businesses and the attempt to control and curtail the social impulse will be justified in terms of the rights of those who would otherwise suffer, rather than the rights of those on whom the burden of regulation falls. If people, in exercising their free choice, set up all-male clubs, then the state is entitled to close those clubs down, or compel them to admit women. For all-male clubs, which create networks of influence that give advantages to men, infringe upon the general right of women to be 'treated as an equal', a right that, according to the liberal jurist Ronald Dworkin, trumps the right to equal treatment, which is the only right that the males who founded the club can, in their conflict with feminist orthodoxy, rely upon.[62] If people refuse to recognize the legitimacy of homosexual unions, or try to exclude homosexuals from their places of work or education, then the

---

62 See Ronald Dworkin's original statement of this position, 'The DeFunis Case: the Right to go to Law School', in *New York Review of Books*, February 1976.

state is entitled to step in and force them to change their ways. For that is what the 'right to be treated as an equal' demands.

The aggregation fallacy helps this kind of argument. For it enables people to believe that they are including both liberty and equality among their goals. There is no need to examine how the one goal qualifies the other, for all goods aggregate in the final account. By advancing the cause of equality we are propagating liberties, since that is what rights really are. Hence you can be a liberal and devote yourself to destroying the liberties that stand in the way of equality. And the state is the most powerful of all the instruments ever devised for doing this. The state can seize the assets of the successful and redistribute them to those who otherwise might fail. It can prevent the formation of exclusive networks and hierarchies and in general control associations, so as to protect those whom they exclude. Hence, in the name of 'treating as an equal', we can impose any kind of unequal treatment and still be upholding the rights and freedoms of the people as a whole.

However, there is another side to it. Many egalitarians remain wedded to the aggregation fallacy, since it allows them to believe that by pursuing equality they are pursuing liberty in its *true* form. They admit that individual freedom is an ultimate good, but interpret freedom in a new way, as bestowed by the 'struggle' for equality. The freedoms advocated by conservatives and individualists are, in the eyes of many egalitarians, forms of 'domination', ways in which one person can exercise power over another. Hence they are only falsely described as liberties. The pursuit of liberty in its true form involves the rooting out of domination. And domination shows itself in many ways – including the ways in which people seek to control each other through custom and law. Hence at the same time as campaigning for an expansion of the state in the public sphere, the new kind of liberal will often campaign for the exclusion of the state from the private sphere, arguing that individuals should be 'liberated' from all attempts to enforce morality through law, or to privilege any particular lifestyle as normative.

When Adam Smith made freedom central to his vision of the modern economy, he was clear that freedom and morality are two sides of a coin. A free society is a community of responsible beings, bound by the laws of sympathy and by the obligations of family love. It is not a society of people released from all moral constraint, for that is precisely the opposite of a society. Without moral constraint there can be no cooperation, no family commitment, no long-term prospects, no hope of economic, let alone social, order. Yet those who describe themselves as 'liberal' wish to chase moral constraints from the law and from every other place in which they might find an enduring foothold in society. They are frequently immoralists in sexual matters, and believe that the state has no business imposing, through the law or the public education system, any particular vision of moral order or spiritual fulfilment. This approach is fortified by the born free fallacy that I discussed in Chapter Three, which provides an exculpating approach to morality that facilitates the transfer of responsibility to the state. In this way is shaped the new liberal agenda: state control over all aspects of public life; total liberation in the private sphere. Whether a society so constituted can survive, and whether it can reproduce itself, are as yet open questions, to which a pessimist will give, as likely as not, a negative answer. Yet the ability of liberal reformers to ignore the signs of social decay, and to press on with the pursuit of their agenda, is not the least remarkable proof that they live in a world of false hopes.

Another example here presents itself. Since the sixties Western countries have adopted policies in the matter of immigration that no person schooled in the elementary truths of pessimism would have endorsed. Anybody who has studied the fate of empires, and the difficulties of establishing territorial jurisdiction over communities that differ in religion, language and marital customs, knows that the task is all but impossible, and threatens constantly to break down in fragmentation, tribalism or civil war. Take the lid off multi-ethnic and multicultural empires – such as the Ottoman Empire or communist Yugoslavia – and bloodshed and destruction immediately ensue. There are remedies, of course, and diplomatic resources, such as those practised so effectively by the Lebanese until Hafez al-Assad's attempt to impose a Syrian empire.[63] But the known results of human peace-making warn us against setting widely different cultures in a single territory.

63   I have examined this tragic example in *A Land Held Hostage: Lebanon and the West*, London, 1987.

The optimistic response to the problems posed by mass immigration was the policy of multiculturalism. Each culture, its advocates argued, is a good in itself. Each has something to offer, whether the joyful festivals of the Hindus, the carnivals of the West Indians, the close-knit families of the Muslims, the quiet industry of the Chinese. Each culture must be given maximum space to grow and fulfil itself, to provide its members with the fruits of social cooperation, and to enjoy the endorsement of an education system that refrains from dictating what can be thought or done or said, but instead awaits guidance from the families that make use of it. In order to offer space to minority cultures, however, the majority culture must be marginalized. It can no longer be allowed to dictate the form and content of the school curriculum, and any suggestion that the place where we are must take precedence over the place that we came from must be carefully excised from the syllabus.

The fallacy here is blatant. All cultures bestow benefits on the people who grow in them, and cultures that have stood the test of time thereby give proof of their virtues. But it does not follow that these many forms of the good can be aggregated. On the contrary, as is made clear by the history of India under the Moguls and the history of the Indian subcontinent today, the presence in one place of two violently opposed forms of life has been the source of continued instability, has led to partitions and civil conflict, and continues to threaten the country with violence. If there is, relatively speaking, peace in India today, it is thanks to the concerted effort of both Hindus and Muslims to put their differences aside, and to create another culture – an overarching civic culture, in which territory, history, law and political institutions are the defining features of civil loyalty.

Just such a culture was the one that we in Britain inherited at the end of the Second World War. It was based on national identity, on a specific Christian inheritance, and above all on the political and legal framework that had made elementary freedoms available to the ordinary subject. Although the Anglican Church had retained its social and political centrality, our schools were full of non-conformists, Jews and agnostic humanists of a somewhat Victorian kind. The public culture of Britain was, so to speak, downstream from Christianity, and downstream also from the Enlightenment. Its most important aspect was contained in the virtues of citizenship, patriotism and obedience to the rule of law. And all these were celebrated in our history books, in our children's literature and in the shape of the school curriculum. To say that Britain was 'monocultural' is to misunderstand the nature of such a national culture, which is always a syncretic concoction out of elements that are both home-grown and imported. The school curriculum that I enjoyed in the fifties and early sixties was in no sense 'ethnocentric'; nor was it focused on the British imperial experience, important though that was in our history lessons. Our curriculum paid great attention to ancient authors in Greek and Latin; to medieval and Renaissance literature in English; to the Hebrew Bible and biblical history, as well as to the gods and heroes of Greece and Rome. We got a fair dose of continental literature, both French and German, and T. S. Eliot was somehow in the air (he had briefly been a master at my grammar school), urging us to read everything mentioned in the footnotes to *The Waste Land*, from Jessie L. Weston's study of medieval vegetation cults to the *Bhagavad Gita*. As for basic beliefs, these were few and imprecise. We were assumed to be Christians, unless we were Jews. But more important than any theological doctrine or ritual practice was the thing called *character*, which showed itself in honest, open dealings with others, in a freedom of manner and a punctilious attention to duties. Our culture was that of the 'law-abiding Englishman'. And the few boys of Indian extraction in our classes hadn't the slightest problem with that.

Multiculturalism did not replace that curriculum; it merely destroyed it. For the advocates of multiculturalism hadn't the faintest idea what they really meant by the term. They believed that we must see 'other cultures' as inherently good, and therefore make room for them, adding them one by one to the curriculum and thereby constantly improving it. But you don't teach cultures in that way. Even if anthropologists have the skill required to hop from one culture to another, taking an overview of each, they can do this because theirs is an *outside* view. But what we value in a culture is the *inside* view – the view of the participants, whose emotions, attachments and goals are all clarified by their immersion in a shared way of life, and the web of rituals and images that has been woven into it.[64] This inside view can be taught, but only by a process of acculturation, in which the one culture is put across as 'ours'. Acculturation is valuable as the precursor to the 'we' attitude – the thing that makes it possible to look on yourself as one among many, with a destiny that is shared. In this sense you cannot learn many cultures. The best you can do is to learn a kind of synthesis of the public culture that you share with your neighbours and the private culture that endures at home. That is exactly what our old 'monocultural' curriculum imparted: a public culture of good behaviour and shared national loyalty, within which the private variations could seek, and find, a home. It was an instrument of peace among strangers, a way of attaching the many different ways of life that flourish on British soil to the territory that they share. And all that multiculturalism has achieved is to disestablish that shared and public culture, to remove its legitimacy and its right to our respect, and to put a great yawning emptiness in its stead. Young people from the minorities, who are looking for a place in the surrounding social order and whose hopes depend on being a part of it, are deprived of the means to belong to any 'we' other than that remembered in the family – and often remembered in idyllic and unrealistic terms, as a blessed sanctuary to which we wanderers will one day return.

I suspect that the dangers of this situation have become apparent even to the optimists who created it. Nobody should really be

---

64 A point familiar from the writings of Ruth Benedict, among many others. See *Patterns of Culture*, London, 1934.

surprised that the young Muslims who blew themselves up in London in the summer of 2005, killing some fifty innocent people, were home-grown British citizens, of immigrant extraction – the first products of the multicultural madness, brought up to regard the surrounding order as one to which they do not and cannot belong, and with a vision of culture derived merely from negating all that their home country has to offer.

However, this brings me to the point of my discussion. Our societies have entered a period of instability and threat. They have been brought to this pass by ways of thinking that are clearly both irrational and compulsive. The fallacies involved in those ways of thinking can be easily exposed. But the thinking remains. What then should we do, and how might we protect ourselves from the false hopes of the deceivers, and acquire true hopes of our own? This is the question that I address in my final three chapters. And I begin by analysing some of the strategies whereby truth has been, and will be, excluded from the discussion.

NINE

Defences Against the Truth

Comprehensive pessimists, whose pessimism deprives the world of its smiling aspect, and who refuse to be cheered by anything, not even by the prospect of their own final extinction, are unattractive characters – unattractive to others, and also to themselves. Truly cheerful people, however, who love life and are grateful for the gift of it, have great need of pessimism, in doses small enough to be digestible, but astute enough to target the follies that surround them, which otherwise poison their joys. They will recoil from the fallacies that I have discussed in this book, and seek to undermine the hold of those fallacies on those who fall for them. They will be troubled by the spectacle of false hope, wanting to bring hope, like faith and charity, to earth and to clothe it in human garments. They will recognize the expansive 'I' attitude for what it is, a desire to remake the world as the compliant servant of a weak and un-self-knowing ego. And they will seek a world in which the 'we' attitude can grow, bringing with it the comforts of genuine society and the free association of reasonable beings.

In short, truly cheerful people will be concerned to defend the truths from which the unscrupulous optimist turns away. They will urge responsibility and accountability in our dealings with each other, and insist that the cost of every risk be borne by the one who takes it. They will insist that, in all thinking about the future, the best case be balanced by a consideration of the worst. In the face of large-scale folly they will urge the claims of small-scale wisdom. Confronted by comprehensive plans for the betterment of mankind, and the associated assaults on tradition, authority and order in all their tried and imperfect forms, they will urge restraint and caution, hoping to protect the space in which the 'we' attitude can flourish. But, if anything were to amplify pessimism and deprive it of its cheerful aspect, it would be the response of the optimists themselves, who are unable to relinquish their illusions. Rather than retrace their steps to discover the fallacies that have engendered their beliefs, the optimists will attack their critics, often with a venom that is hard to endure. Or they will return to their schemes and theories with a renewed enthusiasm, saying that they have not gone far enough, that what is needed is more planning, more liberation, more progress – and more executions.

Certain strategies are habitually used in this defensive action, and it is worth examining them, since they show the way in which human beings conspire to avoid the truth, whenever the truth requires a painful change in routines. First, there is the strategy of onus-shifting. Common sense would suggest that, when you propose some major innovation, promising huge benefits, that the onus is on you to show the likelihood that those benefits will ensue. Invariably, however, the unscrupulous optimist confronts criticism with an onus-shifting argument, saying it is up to you, the cautious pessimist, to prove that the customs and traditions that I condemn really do make a contribution to the common good. Of course, common sense also says that a custom that has survived the test of time has at least this much to be said for it: that it is not dysfunctional. But that does not satisfy the optimists, who insist that you show conclusively that the traditional arrangement is more beneficial than their 'improvement'.

The onus-shifting argument has been used to great effect in the debates over divorce and abortion. Those who said that making divorce easier would threaten the stability of marriage and the interests of children were faced by a challenge to prove the point, and also to disprove the claim of their opponents, that easy divorce would ensure that good marriages last, and bad marriages come quickly to an end. How do you prove such things? Deprive common sense and custom of their authority and you can prove anything or nothing, depending on your starting point. Ronald Dworkin told us that it is for the opponent of abortion 'rights' to show that the damage done by permitting them exceeds the damage to the mental health of women that comes from forbidding them.[65] And of course no such thing could be *proved* in advance – even though in retrospect, witnessing the genocidal scale of abortions in America and the careless attitude to parenting that now prevails, it is tempting to say that no proof was needed. Unscrupulous optimists tell us that it is for those who defend the old marital customs to prove that gay marriage will threaten an established social good, and not for those who propose this innovation to show that it will leave the good of marriage undiminished.

All conservatives have had to deal with the onus-shifting argument, which effectively gives a head start to innovation, however unjustified, and however destabilizing. The residues of collective reasonableness in custom, tradition and the common law, in which the solutions to countless conflicts and difficulties have sedimented to provide a fertile soil of precedents, are made to count for nothing in the face of innovations that have little to recommend them apart from the hope and excitement of their proponents. In this way 'I' drives out 'we' without a battle.

But there are other defences that have been equally important in securing optimistic schemes against doubt. I consider four of them: false expertise, transferred blame, hermeticism and scapegoating. I give examples of each strategy in order to illustrate the general principles involved. Even if the examples belong to our time, it should not be thought that there is anything new in the

---

65   See Ronald Dworkin, *Life's Dominion: an Argument about Abortion, Euthanasia and Individual Freedom*, New York, 1992.

phenomena they illustrate. It is well known that Apollo, in bestowing the gift of prophecy on Cassandra, also punished her rejection of his advances by ensuring that no one would ever believe her warnings. And such is the fate of the Old Testament prophets too. However cautious pessimists may be, they will constantly find themselves confronted by strategies designed to thwart or ridicule their warnings, and it is only in rare cases that they can win through to a victory for common sense. Why this is so will be the topic of the chapter that follows. That it is so is illustrated by the examples below.

First, then, false expertise. The strategy is to invent experts, backed up by all the apparatus of scholarship, research and 'peer review', and provided with concepts and agendas that make it virtually impossible to put a spoke in their wheel. This is a long-standing strategy, which goes back to the beginnings of the modern university in the Christian and Muslim communities of the Middle Ages. Theology – which is a very different discipline in Cairo's Al-Azhar University from that taught in the Catholic University of Milan – was the foundational discipline of our universities. It produced great works of philosophy, history and biblical scholarship. But it was, and is, entirely phoney. The purpose of theology has been to generate experts about a topic concerning which there are no experts, namely God. Built into every version of theology are the foregone conclusions of a faith: conclusions that are not to be questioned but only surrounded with fictitious scholarship and secured against disproof.

We should not regret the centrality of theology in the old university; it had spin-offs in philosophy, literature and the natural sciences for which we should all be grateful. In Aquinas's *Summa* we see how the attempt to secure faith against doubt produces the most majestic exploration of doubt in all its aspects, and a brilliant exposition of the distinguishing marks of the human condition. The same cannot be said for the subjects that have recently grown from the same basic principle – subjects like women's studies, gender studies, gay studies and peace studies, designed to bury a foregone conclusion in a mound of pseudo-scholarship. Perhaps the most interesting and influential such subject in our time has been that of 'education'. This was invented as an academic discipline in order to find endorsement for the new vision of the school as a place for producing social equality, rather than for reproducing knowledge. The experts in education were supposed to know all about the psychology, philosophy and sociology of schooling, and about the real – and hitherto misunderstood – significance of education in a modern society. But they were not required to have any first-hand knowledge of a subject, or any real standing in any previously acknowledged discipline. Even though they were incompetent to step into a classroom and impart the knowledge that the pupils were there to acquire, they were the 'experts' in all matters to do with the process of acquiring it.

Whenever decisions had to be made about schooling, curriculum and teacher training it was the 'educationists' who were consulted – often people who had shown so little ability to acquire knowledge of a real discipline that they had decided to learn how to teach it instead. Their agenda was uniformly egalitarian, child-centred and knowledge-averse, and it is thanks largely to the educationists that the born free fallacy was inserted at the very foundation of educational reform in Britain, continental Europe and America. The fact that the educationists knew nothing of real significance was never counted as a disadvantage. On the contrary, it freed their minds for the far greater task of removing from the curriculum all those obstacles to false hope that had been planted there by previous generations of scholars: obstacles like Latin, calculus, counterpoint and national history, all of which I was taught at school, and all of which have since been effectively removed from the school curriculum.

Invented expertise has been equally useful in shoring up the false hopes that have accompanied the sexual revolution. A short while ago in England a two-year-old baby, known then as Baby P, died after eight months of systematic torture from his mother and her boyfriend. Social workers and paediatricians had had the case on their books, but been unable, unwilling or legally incompetent to act. So horrifying were the injuries to the child that his plight made headline news, and the subsequent trial and conviction of the mother and two men for 'causing or allowing' Baby P's death was the nationwide drama of the day. However, in all the discussions that ensued, the principal theme was that of child abuse, and the experts appointed to diagnose and rectify it. These experts have powers to advise the courts, which can make orders to remove children from the care of their parents and see to their adoption in some institution under the auspices of the state. The first response to the case of Baby P was to describe these experts as overworked and underfunded, implying that more of them were needed. The concept of 'child abuse', on which a vast bureaucracy has been erected throughout the Western world, and which automatically suggests a complex social and psychological condition with which only experts are able to deal, gained a further hold on public opinion and the machinery of government. What is needed, the experts insisted, is more of *us*, more planning, more supervision, more ways of preventing this society-wide disorder through the intervention of a benevolent state.

Actually what Baby P needed was a father, and the smallest dose of pessimism would have pointed this out. The Family Education Trust has demonstrated that children are thirty-three times more likely to suffer serious abuse and seventy-three times more likely to suffer fatal abuse in the home of a mother with a live-in boyfriend or stepfather than in an intact family.[66] Fathers instinctively protect their children. Boyfriends, for whom another man's child is a rival, instinctively attack them. If we think in this way, however, we find ourselves confronting one of the fundamental prejudices of the time: the prejudice that the new forms of domestic life brought about by easy divorce and the sexual

66   Robert Whelan, *Broken Homes & Battered Children: A study of the relationship between child abuse and family type*, Oxford, 1994.

revolution are unalterable and unquestionable. Child abuse is not a universal social disorder, for which the state bureaucracy and its experts are the cure. It is the direct result of the delegitimization of the family, often carried out by those very experts. Meanwhile, the state has connived in the dissolution of the marriage tie, and has routinely subsidized, through the welfare system, the arrangements (including live-in boyfriends) that expose children to danger. Furthermore, thanks to the experts, it is standard practice in divorce cases for judges to award custody of the child to the mother, so depriving children of their principal protector.

All that I have written in that paragraph would be either dismissed as the prejudice of an old fogey or attacked as harsh, discriminatory and oppressive by the experts who have been appointed to decide these matters. Examine their expertise, however, and whence it derives, and you will discover a mishmash of amateur sociology, left-wing dogma and routinized anti-family rhetoric.[67] Yet the government's report into the case of Baby P, conducted by Lord Laming, perpetuates the view that, if there is a problem, it is with the child protection services, which need to be 'retrained', washed in a new shower of expertise and, of course, better funded. The cause of the problem, which is the erosion of the family at the hands of the state, is unmentionable.

Political correctness is not the only reason for this response. The strategy of transferred blame also has a part to play.

67 See Stephen Baskerville, *Taken into Custody: The War against Fathers, Marriage and the Family*, London, 2007.

Unscrupulous optimists, faced with a real obstacle to their plans, will not as a rule blame the forces that created that obstacle; they will blame whatever can be readily changed, whatever responds to blame. That way they secure a simple avenue to improvements. You cannot easily restore the institution of the family; you cannot, without confrontation, penalize single mothers, fathers who abandon their children, or sexual mores that leave children to their own devices. But you can change the social services; you can demand more and better 'experts'; you can increase funding and reallocate resources. That this will do no conceivable good is beside the point: it exemplifies the first principle of bureaucratic government, encapsulated in the order 'don't just stand there, do something!'.

The strategy of transferred blame is better illustrated, however, by an example from a previous crisis, that which gave rise to the Peace Movement, surely one of the most interesting cases of misplaced optimism in modern history. This movement is not new. It was anticipated by the 'Peace Pledge Union', initiated by Dick Sheppard, Canon of St Paul's, in 1934, which was a major force in delaying British rearmament in the face of Hitler. The Union promoted the view that war is caused by our preparations for it, and that it suffices to change our ways, to avoid belligerent gestures and to show in everything our peace-loving aspect and the threat of hostilities will disappear. This paradigmatically optimistic view, which ought to have been refuted by the war that followed, has continually returned to dominate the stance of forward-looking people towards the threats presented by the modern world. Its most striking manifestation in recent times has been the 'peace offensive' launched by the Soviet Union in 1980, shortly after its invasion of Afghanistan. Through front organizations such as the Transnational Institute in Amsterdam and the World Council of Churches in Prague, the KGB was able to use the existing peace movements to orchestrate a response favourable to Soviet strategy. In particular it was vital to Soviet strategy to retain the power to subjugate Europe, and to prevent the deployment of the Cruise missiles that were to be the cornerstone of NATO's defence against invasion.

Without going into the rights and wrongs of the NATO response or the policies pursued by CND and its allegedly more circumspect offshoot END (the European campaign for Nuclear Disarmament), we should recognize the importance for the peace movement as a whole of the strategy of transferred blame. Even the most unscrupulous of the optimists involved was aware that protests of the kind organized by CND (such as the camp of 'peace-loving' women at Greenham Common, one of the bases chosen for the deployment of the Cruise missiles) were impossible in the Soviet Empire, where all dissent was instantly suppressed. Everyone was aware that it was futile to blame the Soviet leaders – not because they were not to blame, but because blame served no purpose when addressing a machine that had cancelled *ab origine* the very possibility of responding to criticism. Yet the desire to blame remained, and the hope, along with it, that blame would serve a purpose – that it would so alter things as to avert the threat of war. A clear solution to the problem presented itself, namely to blame the threats of the enemy on our strategy of matching them.

Thus arose the doctrine that war is caused by weapons, and that by arming ourselves against attack we expose ourselves to far more danger than by maintaining an army of ceremonial cavalry. That was the doctrine of the peace movement, which was widely adopted on the left. It coincided with the official Soviet position, which was that, in any war involving communists, it is those who resist communist takeover who are the aggressors. The movement gave rise to a culture of capitulation not unlike that which arose in response to Hitler's rearmament. It involved initiatives such as the 'peace studies' movement – a false expertise strategy that targeted schools and universities all over Western Europe, to present the fundamental doctrine on which the movement was built, the doctrine that to deter attack is actually to invite it, as the foundational principle of an academic discipline. In the event, as we know, the peace movement did not succeed, and President Reagan's strategy of deterrence helped to bring about the collapse of the Soviet Union and the liberation of Eastern Europe. But the strategy of transferred blame remained in place and has been active in fortifying spurious optimisms ever since. It is another of the roots of contemporary anti-Americanism, which thrives in large part because, in all the conflicts and strategies in which it is involved, the United States is alone responsive to criticism.

This is why, following the attacks of 9/11, there was an immediate explosion of blame directed at America. Everybody knew – and the nature of the attacks sufficiently demonstrated this – that al-Qaeda is not an organization with which dialogue is possible, or which is in the habit of examining its conscience and regretting its acts. It exists to recruit resentment and to direct that resentment against the usual target, which is the one who is at home in the world and who enjoys the fruits that we the resentful have failed to harvest. What is the point of blaming such an organization, or even making moral judgements? No, let us turn instead to America and see what she has done – through her very success – to *deserve* these strikes. Immediately after the destruction of the Twin Towers, Ward Churchill wrote an essay in the *Daily Camera*, 'Some People Push Back', in which he borrowed the phrase previously used by John Zerzan in his justification of the Unabomber's random murders. The phrase was 'little Eichmanns', used to compare the 3,000 people who died in the Twin Towers to the Nazi concentration-camp commander who was eventually captured and brought to trial in Jerusalem. The article was naturally the subject of intense controversy at the time. But many rushed to justify the description, and to insist that it did nothing more than underline the inbuilt blameworthiness of America. The attacks, however regrettable, were the inevitable and to-be-expected result of US policies. And in describing the victims as 'little Eichmanns', Churchill had merely emphasized the special role of financial institutions in the American imperial machine.

The readiness to transfer blame in this way is fortified by the attitude that Nietzsche called *ressentiment*. When bad things happen, especially when they happen to me, I have a motive to seek the person, group or collective that caused them and on whom they can be blamed. And the zero sum fallacy steps in to suggest that the proof of guilt lies in success. In every conflict, therefore, we should blame the party that enjoys the advantage. This strategy is particularly rewarding in the case of the United States, where a dynamic community, enjoying a free press and a continuous public debate, makes room for criticism in a way that is not to be observed anywhere else in the world. So we should not be surprised to find that anti-Americanism is an immediate response to any conflict that involves America, and that its most virulent manifestations are in America itself. The more America is attacked, the more she will be targeted by her own internal critics. Only the reduction of the USA to poverty and impotence would finally silence people like Howard Zinn and Noam Chomsky: not because that is what they want, but because only then would blame be redundant.

I mention those last two thinkers not only because of their enormous influence in recent years, but also because they illustrate the way in which transferred blame in general, and the anti-American version of it in particular, have been useful in defending false hopes from refutation. In the wake of the sixties, the revolutionary worldview, which is built upon the fallacies that I have outlined in this work, enjoyed an unprecedented triumph among thinking people. It was sufficient to preface your credo with a criticism of Stalinism, and few would dissent from the remainder, however many absurdities it might contain concerning the emancipation of the proletariat, the withering away of the state or the overthrow of bourgeois 'domination'. Look at the writings of Sartre, contained in *Situations*, which coincided with the Vietnam War, and you will quickly perceive the utility of anti-Americanism in permitting that great thinker to turn a blind eye to the history of the revolutionary doctrines that he defended. Something similar occurred later with the disaster of Cambodia, when Chomsky (a thinker every bit as important in his way as Sartre) was able to dismiss the reports of Pol Pot's atrocities as a *New York Times* fabrication. Throughout those crucial years in which the communist threat had seldom, in fact, been more alarming, with the Soviet Union and China fomenting unrest and undermining governments throughout Asia, Africa and the Middle East, and when the US alone was attempting to counter what might have been a worldwide disaster, the Western intellectuals were enjoying an orgy of anti-Americanism, and the leading anti-Americans were fêted wherever they chose to speak – and nowhere more than in the universities of America.

I do not say that their criticisms were entirely wrong. On the contrary, they often hit the mark. But this occasional truthfulness was a side-effect that had no bearing on the hidden purpose, which was not to discover the truth about ourselves, but to conceal the truth about our enemy. The anti-Americans recognized no opposing viewpoint, acknowledged no virtue in an American political system that permitted them to criticize it from within, while enjoying every established privilege and never inviting their opponents to a debate. Their purpose was to conceal the truth about revolutionary politics, about socialism, about liberation movements and terrorist tactics that, if it were better known, would justify a great many of the interventions that America has attempted.

The third truth-avoiding strategy is one that has had such an impact on universities that the real questions confronting modern societies are seldom now debated at the academic level. The strategy involves not defending one's position, but concealing it within a fortified citadel of nonsense, of a kind designed to accuse the critic of ignorance or lack of logical skill. Of course nonsense has found a home in the academy almost from the time when Plato started it. But it has also been the target of satire: from Abelard and Averroës to Schopenhauer and Lewis Carroll academic incoherence has been lampooned from within the academy with the same verve as it has been scoffed at by the rest of us.

In the sixties, however, a wholly new kind of nonsense came on the scene, produced by radical gurus for the consumption of the revolutionary young. This brand-new species of nonsense was almost instantly adopted by the professors – who were not to be outdone in revolutionary zeal by their students – and made into the foundation of the postmodern curriculum. From that moment on the most appalling intellectual confusions could be propagated in the universities and – provided only that they appeared impeccably left-wing in their implications – were immediately set beyond criticism.

Like most revolutions, it began in Paris. The young revolutionaries whom I knew in 1968 were obsessed by Louis Althusser, whose *Pour Marx* reads like a liturgical invocation of the Devil, composed by someone who is lifting uncomprehended phrases from a poor translation of *Das Kapital*. Here is a representative passage:

> This is not just its situation *in principle* (the one it occupies in the hierarchy of instances in relation to the determinant instance: in society, the economy) nor just its situation *in fact* (whether, in the phase under consideration, it is dominant or subordinate) but *the relation of this situation in fact to this situation in principle*, that is, the very relation which makes of this situation in fact a *variation of the – 'invariant' – structure, in dominance, of the totality.*

Pour Marx is composed entirely of such boxes of fortified emptiness. It is not surprising that Althusser's disciples could agree, at the time, only on the meaning of the title: Althusser was very definitely for Marx, not against him. Alas, had he been against Marx, he would have been greeted with the derision that he deserved. As it is, he was at once adopted as a foundational authority of the new curriculum, someone whose work it became instantly imperative to discuss. Its very incomprehensibility was a guarantee of its relevance. Only someone who had 'seen through all the pretences' could write like that!

In the wake of Althusser a torrent of gobbledygook came streaming from the womb of history, which at that time was situated in the Left Bank journal *Tel Quel*. This journal published essays by Derrida, Kristeva, Sollers, Deleuze, Guattari and a thousand more, all of them manufacturers of junk thought, only one aspect of which was clearly meant to be understood, namely its character as revolutionary 'subversion'. Their vatic style, in which words are cast as spells rather than used as arguments, inspired innumerable imitators in humanities departments across the Western world. At last, anybody could be a thinker! It was no longer necessary to have an idea of your own, or to have studied how to express real thought and emotion in careful words. You could just write like this:

Within that conflictual economy of colonial discourse which Edward Said describes as the tension between the synchronic panoptical vision of domination – the demand for identity, stasis – and the counterpressure of the diachrony of history – change, difference – mimicry represents an *ironic* compromise. If I may adapt Samuel Weber's formulation of the marginalizing vision of castration...

Or like this:

> The rememoration of the 'present' as space is the possibil-
> ity of the utopian imperative of no-(particular)-place, the
> metropolitan project that can supplement the post-colonial
> attempt at the impossible cathexis of place-bound history
> as the lost time of the spectator...

Those two quotations from people who hold distinguished chairs in Ivy League universities illustrate what has become the lingua franca of the humanities: gibberish with side-swipes. In their important work, *Fashionable Nonsense*, Alan Sokal and Jean Bricmont have taken some of this nonsense apart.[68] But to no avail. Even the spoof article published by Sokal in *Social Text*, deliberately designed to expose the intellectual fraudulence of the new subversive idiom, has left the intellectual landscape unchanged. The nonsense has been piled too high to yield to a spade, however energetically used. In any case Sokal and Bricmont, who identify themselves as leftists disappointed with the intellectual betrayal of their beliefs, fail to see that leftism is what it is all about. The best way to create a left-wing orthodoxy in the academy is to fortify the leftist position with armoured nonsense: for then criticism becomes impossible.

68 Alan Sokal and Jean Bricmont, *Fashionable Nonsense: Postmodern Intellectuals' Abuse of Science*, New York, 1998, published as *Intellecual Impostures in Britain*, London, 1997.

It seems to me that it is only as leftists that writers like Derrida, Kristeva and their more recent successors such as Luce Irigaray and Hélène Cixous should be read. And their nonsense, footnoted and referenced in a thousand academic journals – the *Modern Language Review* being the most influential – has now been deposited in Augean quantities over every available space of the curriculum. The result of this concerted effort to make the leftist position impregnable has been an intellectual disaster, one comparable to the burning of the library at Alexandria, or the closing of the schools of Greece.

And the disaster continues. Young people may have little time, now, for the 'theories' of the Parisian gurocracy; but their ageing teachers, who have made their careers with articles on Derrida's somewhat too convenient proof that meaning is impossible and all language metaphor (yes: literally!) or Irigaray's equally important proof that $E = MC^2$ is a 'sexed equation', have nothing else to offer them. Truth, validity and knowledge were driven from the curriculum by the sacred texts of the postmodern curriculum, and nonsense put in their place. And behind that nonsense lies the ever mischievous promise of liberation – liberation not from truth and reason only, but from the very thought of the human community as something more important than yourself.

This, it seems to me, is one of the most interesting forms of false hope to have emerged in recent times. Professors in the humanities learned from their French mentors that there is a way of writing that will always be considered 'profound', provided only that it is (a) subversive and (b) unintelligible. As long as a text can be read as in some way *against* the status quo of Western culture and society, undermining its claim to authority or truth, it does not matter that it is gibberish. On the contrary, that is merely a proof that its argument operates at a level of profundity that makes it immune to criticism.

It is, of course, not only modern leftism that has had recourse to the hermetic strategy by way of protecting its illusions. The original discipline of theology was prodigal of nonsense, and the hermetic science of alchemy provided a more secular version of it, which Ben Jonson adequately satirized in *The Alchemist*. Whenever impossible aims and unbelievable doctrines take up position in the human psyche, offering spurious hopes and factitious solutions, gobbledygook assembles in the wings, awaiting its moment. All revolutions make use of it; and there is hardly a religion that does not have its fellow-travelling mystics, whose role is to protect the message by making it unintelligible. But religions have another and more effective defence, which is the charge of heresy and the punishments that such a charge invites. Nor is it only religions that defend themselves in this way, and it is fitting to conclude this chapter with a modern instance, since it bears on the great silence that lies at the heart of modern communities, whose principal problem has become undiscussable.

'Human kind cannot bear very much reality,' said T. S. Eliot. It is not one of his best lines, but he used it twice – in *Murder in the Cathedral* and in *Four Quartets* – and in both places its prosaic

rhythmlessness reinforces its sense, reminding us that our exalta-
tions are invented things, and that we prefer inspiring fantasies to
sobering facts. Enoch Powell was no different, and his inspiring
fantasy of England caused him to address his countrymen as
though they still enjoyed the benefits of a classical education and
an imperial culture. How absurd, in retrospect, to end a speech
(delivered to the Birmingham Conservatives in 1968) warning
against the effects of uncontrolled immigration with a concealed
quotation from Virgil. 'As I look ahead,' Powell said, 'I am filled
with foreboding. Like the Roman, I seem to see "the River Tiber
foaming with much blood".' These words were addressed to an
England that had forgotten the story of the *Aeneid*, along with
every other story woven into its former identity as the 'sweet, just,
boyish master' of the world – to borrow Santayana's luminous
phrase.[69] It is hardly surprising that Powell's words were instantly
converted to 'rivers of blood', and their speaker dismissed as a
dangerous madman. However, Powell's speech and the reaction to
it are worthy of study here, since they illustrate the way in which,
in moments of strain, when the illusions of the optimist are in
danger of refutation, the critic is recast as the enemy within. He is
not the one who is arguing for a rival position. He is the one who
stands out from the crowd as a sacrificial victim. He is the scapegoat, whose ruination is joyfully undertaken, as the much needed
proof that my illusions are invulnerable, since they are *shared*.

69 George Santayana, 'The British Character', in *Soliloquies in England and
Later Soliloquies*, London, 1922.

It is, in fact, the Cumean Sibyl who utters that prophecy in Book VI of the *Aeneid*, and although she is foreseeing the troubles that come from immigration, it is to the troubles suffered by an immigrant that she refers. The immigrant in question – Aeneas – travels to Italy at the head of a determined retinue, carrying his household gods and a divine right of residence. His intention to settle is not to be brooked, and if this means 'wars, horrid wars', so be it. Modern immigrants don't, on the whole, behave so badly. They don't need to. Yet, like Aeneas, our immigrants come carrying their household gods. Like Aeneas, they come with an unbrookable intention to make a home for themselves. And if their gods dislike the indigenous rivals, they will soon make this fact known. Such predictions as Powell made in his speech, concerning the tipping of the demographic balance, the ghettoization of the industrial cities and the growth of resentment among the indigenous working class, have been fulfilled.[70] Only the sibylline prophecy has fallen short of the mark. Even so, the Madrid and London bombings and the murder of Theo Van Gogh are viewed by many Europeans as a foretaste of things to come. It is now evident that, in the debate over immigration, in those last remaining days when it could still have made a difference, Enoch Powell was far nearer the truth than those who instantly drove him from office, and who ensured that the issue was henceforth to be discussed, if at all, only by way of condemning the 'racism'

70   See Geoff Dench and Kate Gavron, *Lost Horizons*, London, 2006.

and 'xenophobia' of those who thought like Powell. As for the racism and xenophobia of the incomers, it was indiscernible to the liberal conscience, which has never been able to understand that liberalism is an *unusual state of mind*.

At the time when Powell made his speech many British politicians were schooled in the Bible and the Greek and Roman classics; they could dispute the factual basis for Powell's prophecy only by putting out of mind what they had every reason to know, namely that many of the newcomers to Britain would be strangers to liberal values, attached to their own communities, suspicious towards the host culture and anxious to insulate themselves and their children from its influence. In the face of those manifest truths our political class had recourse to Doublethink. Like the White Queen in *Through the Looking Glass*, they practised the art of believing six impossible things before breakfast, including the proposition that pious Muslims from the hinterlands of Asia would produce children loyal to a secular European state.

This flight from reality is not a new feature of political life. It is always easier to bequeath a problem to your successors than to face it yourself, and when the problem is intractable Doublethink will soon erase it, as Hitler was erased from the thoughts of the appeasers, and the Gulag from the political map of the peaceniks. Nor are American presidents any more realistic than the rest of us. When the embassy in Tehran was invaded and US citizens taken hostage, President Carter chose not to notice what was, certainly *de facto* and probably *de jure*, a declaration of war. That may be proved the costliest mistake made by America in the Middle East. Likewise the silencing of Enoch Powell has proved more costly than any other post-war domestic policy in Britain, since it has ensured that immigration can be discussed only now, when it is too late to do anything about it or to confine it to those who come in a spirit of obedience towards the indigenous law.

Of course, Powell himself was also in flight from reality – the reality of British society as it was in 1968. His invocation of Virgil fell on deaf ears, or rather on ears that pricked up only at the sound of 'blood'. His punctilious syntax, resounding with the rhythms of the Book of Common Prayer and rich in allusions to a history that was publicly remembered, if at all, only as an object of ridicule, created the impression of a paterfamilias in some Edwardian play, strutting at the front of the stage while his disobedient daughter flirts unnoticed in the background.

Truth, Plato believed, is the business of philosophy, but it is rhetoric, not philosophy, that moves the crowd. So how can we protect people from fatal errors such as those that tempted Athens into conflict with Sparta, or those that, much later, led the Germans, mesmerized by Hitler, into an equally suicidal war? Plato wanted philosophers to be kings, but he did not believe that they would be listened to: the words of philosophers would sound strange and ambiguous, and their eyes would be turned from present and time-bound emergencies towards the stratosphere of eternal truths. Nevertheless, among the rhetorical devices that would be necessary in government it is still possible to distinguish the noble lies from their ignoble negations. The noble lie is the untruth that conveys a truth, the myth that maps reality. It is thus that Plato justified the stories of the gods and their origins. These stories inspire people to live as though nearer to the source of things, and to discover in themselves the virtues that exist only when we find our way to believing in them.

In the Platonic scheme of things Powell's vision of England might be seen as a noble lie. He was exhorting his countrymen to *live up to* something, and that thing was an ideal image of their country, shaped by myth in the style of Hesiod. The England of Powell's dream was fashioned from heroic deeds and immemorial customs; from sacred rites and solemn offices whose meaning was inscrutable from any point outside the social context that defined them. By fixing their sights on this vision, the British people would be in some way perfecting themselves, and establishing their right to their ancestral territory. In place of this noble vision, however, they were also being offered an ignoble lie. The emerging multicultural community would make no place for a common obedience, a common loyalty or a shared history: it would inevitably deprive the British people of their geographical, cultural and political inheritance. And yet they were being told that it would not harm them, that they would even be improved by it, since it would inject energy, variety and youth into a tired old island.

It was impossible to discern in Powell's steely manner, ancestor-laden syntax and fixed expressionless gaze whether he really believed in the nation that he described with his tone-less incantations. In the end, however, his sincerity and motives became irrelevant. He was cast in the role of the Old Testament prophet – a role that resonated with his name and fitted him for the fate of the scapegoat.[71]

The hounding of Enoch Powell, therefore, took on a righteous character that enabled him to be silenced with an easy conscience, and without addressing the concerns to which he had given voice. Those in the vanguard of the witch-hunt were comfortable voices of the liberal establishment, people who had felt the hurt of Powell's remarks in the visceral centre of their being. They had to make a sacrificial victim of Powell, not because he threatened their material interests but because he threatened something far more important – their illusions.

This illustrates a more general point. Ritual sacrifice can have a redeeming and renewing effect. But this effect comes about because the victim has challenged some aspect of the divinely ordained order of things. His punishment is seen as coming from on high, from the god whose rule he has challenged, and who is now acting to give proof of his reality and righteousness.[72] This is the aspect of ritual sacrifice that has survived into our times, and which we witness most vividly in the Moscow show trials and the 'struggles' of Maoist China, in which the victims enthusiastically

71   See René Girard, *Le bouc émissaire*, Paris, 1982.

72   Such, for example, is the fate of Pentheus in Euripides' *Bacchae*.

confessed to their faults before being executed as though at their own request, like the sacrificial bull of the Greeks, who supposedly nods his head in acquiescence as the axe is about to fall.

The case of Powell illustrates another truth-deflecting stratagem, which is to accuse the victim of the hatred of which he is the target. Those who hounded Powell knew that there was hatred in the air; but they were determined that they themselves were not the cause of it. They were acting to 'stamp out' a hatred that their victim had introduced. And they backed up the charge with the most ugly label that they could attach to him – the label 'racist', which has become in our times the equivalent of 'witch' in seventeenth-century Salem. In all the causes to which unscrupulous optimists attach themselves there is a tendency to accuse opponents of 'hate' and 'hate speech', even though these opponents are the targets of the hatred and not the source of it. Opponents of gay marriage in America regularly receive threatening e-mails denouncing them for the 'hate' that they are propagating.[73] To doubt the equivalence of gay sex and heterosexual marriage is to evince 'homophobia', the moral equivalent of the racism that led to Auschwitz. Likewise, public criticism of Islam and Islamists is a sign of 'Islamophobia', now a crime in Belgian law; and 'hate speech' laws are on the statute books in many European countries, making the mere discussion of issues that are of the greatest concern to our future into a crime. The

73 See the cases assembled (and deplored) by the American organization Gaypatriot on its website (www.gaypatriot.net).

important point here is not the rightness or wrongness of the attitudes accused, but the habit of attributing to the accused the hatred felt by the accuser. This lies deep in the human psyche, and can be witnessed in all the witch-hunts documented by Mackay and others.[74]

Hence, although the examples I have given in this chapter are controversial and close to the bone, it is important to consider them, since they show defensive habits that are still with us. Now, as in the past, these habits serve to divert our collective decisions away from the reasonable scepticism that is needed, and to put false hope in the place of it. Nor is it only optimists who indulge these habits. Whenever a way of life has been built on a false or questionable belief, the defences that I have discussed in this chapter will come to the rescue of the believers. The history of all religions bears witness to this. And even pessimistic worldviews will defend themselves from challenges in a similar way. The more passionate believers in global warming and catastrophic climate change exhibit this trait, advocating false expertise, perpetrating witch-hunts against dissenters like Bjørn Lomborg, and adopting nonsense as a guarantee of profundity.[75] There is

---

74 Charles Mackay, *Extraordinary Popular Delusions and the Madness of Crowds*, London, 1852.

75 A notable example of this nonsense is the so-called 'Precautionary Principle', which forbids everything and therefore nothing, and which is ritually presented as justifying whatever panic the campaigners have become afflicted by. See Roger Scruton, 'The Cult of Precaution', *National Interest*, June 2004.

nothing surprising in this. Science itself, in Thomas Kuhn's well-known account, is reluctant to move to a new 'paradigm', rather than to make whatever adjustments are necessary to save the old one.[76] Nevertheless move it does, and refutation is still the primary instrument of scientific advance. The defences I have discussed in this chapter are designed precisely to shift a belief out of the realm of refutation into the false haven of a way of life. And no haven seems as secure from intellectual storms as the haven of false hopes.

76   Thomas Kuhn, *The Structure of Scientific Revolutions*, London, 1962.

TEN

Our Tribal Past

An age-old device of philosophy, put to powerful use by Bodin, Hobbes, Locke and Rousseau, is the thought-experiment that imagines human beings emerging from a 'state of nature' by joining together in a contract, thereby establishing the institutions of government. The 'social contract' has had an influence out of all proportion to its plausibility as history, since it permits us to represent the obligations of civil society as though they had a beginning and could be spelled out in contractual terms. However, as Hume and Hegel in their very different ways pointed out, the ability to enter into contracts presupposes capacities such as language use, a sense of obligation and recognition of the other that do not exist in a state of nature, and that come into existence only with the comprehensive 'we' of civil society. The traditional philosophical accounts of our primeval origins are myths – ways in which our civilized condition is read back into pre-history, so as to ask what we would look like if we took all civil institutions away.

Rather than construct an imagined 'state of nature', I propose instead to think in more scientific terms about what actually might have happened in the early years of our species, when habits of thought were acquired that were beneficial to our needy ancestors and saw them through those days of hardship. I shall try to imagine how things were when people had not emerged from their tribal groups to form organized societies of strangers, and when contracts and negotiations were hardly known. Consider, then, a small tribe of hunter-gatherers who have moved into new territory in search of food. They have no laws and all disputes are settled by the chieftain, whose title has been established by shows of force. It is to the chieftain that the people look for guidance and leadership, and because their lives are entirely dependent on his favour, they unthinkingly obey him in every emergency. And emergencies there are, not only in the form of wild animals, shortages and inclement weather but also, and more importantly, in the form of competing tribes, one of which is attempting to claim the very same hunting ground. Such a situation does not correspond to the state of nature as described by Hobbes; nor does it contain 'noble savages' of the kind postulated by Rousseau. But it is how our ancestors in the Pleistocene age are often described by those who have considered the evidence.

In such circumstances there is little room for the attitude that looks on our social condition from outside, and encourages collective decision-making and reflection on what is fixed and unalterable in the human state. There is not the safety or the leisure that allows institutions and laws to form, as residues of human agreements. Decisions made for the tribe are made by the chieftain, whose 'I' is also the 'we' of the community. In all fights and hunts it is the chieftain's leadership that is decisive, and the community endures through obedience to his will. Those who ask awkward questions are of no use to such a community, which is engaged in a life-and-death struggle that depends on decisiveness and certainty if it is to be won. The thinking of the chieftain is the thinking of the tribe, and in the conflict with its rivals the tribe needs one thing above all, which is the prior conviction of its own success. A chieftain with doubts is one who is destined to disappear. Only the one who ignores the risk, and boldly stakes out his territory will be a reliable leader, and it is the thinking of such a leader that will be inscribed in the brains that survive.

What in our circumstances might be criticized as the best case fallacy will, in these primeval conditions, be an indispensable habit of mind. In a life-and-death struggle there is no worst case to consider: you either succeed or die; to aim at the best case is the only coherent course of action and to prepare for the worst case is to prepare for nothing. The solution to every strategic problem is confidence, and those who remind the tribe of the cost of failure, which is extinction, add nothing to the collective wisdom other than the paralysing fear of death.

The tribe will act as a single collective 'I', aiming in everything for territory, concerned constantly to increase its scope and confine the scope of its rivals. It will be motivated by a primordial fear of constraints imposed by others. In no sense is the tribe free, as we, thanks to customs and institutions, are free; it will have no ability as yet to enter into negotiations with its rivals, or to settle disputes through law and treaty. Such things come only later, after the life-and-death struggle has been transcended – in something like the way Hegel imagined. This means that the tribe will view consensual order with incomprehension: all it knows is the command of the single 'I', an 'I' internalized by each of its members to become the collective consciousness of the community. The residue of this situation, in the minds of people born into civilized communities, is arguably at the root of the born free fallacy – the sense of an original condition untroubled by compromise, institutions or laws. In that age of innocence there was no 'we' attitude to cancel out the primordial 'I' of tribal conflict, and put negotiation and accountability in its place. There was a guiltless purity and clarity of motive. Of course, that original condition was not one of freedom as I have defended it. It was one of submission – but a submission without the bonds of law and compromise, a primordial innocence in which responsibilities never arose.

Life-and-death struggles are zero-sum games, and everything that affects the collective self-interest of the tribe will be seen in these terms. My loss is the other's gain, and his loss is my gain. The situation has yet to emerge in which I benefit from the benefits of others, and in which we can reach agreements that are good for everyone who enters them. In the primordial struggle, therefore, zero-sum thinking will be the norm. This will be true not only in relations with the enemy, but also in matters of domestic control. In the sharing of booty my gain is always another's loss, and the division of the quarry will be a primary concern of everyone. The one who is given more – whether through strength or as a reward – thereby imposes a burden on the others. And this will be the norm in all distributions conducted under hunter-gatherer circumstances, in which the product is not created but found.

Anthropologists have sometimes traced the egalitarian outlook to the conditions of the hunter-gatherer.[77] I doubt that such speculations are a sufficient explanation of this habit of thought. Nevertheless, we can suppose that in hunter-gatherer conditions zero-sum thinking will be the norm in all conflicts, whether external or internal, and that this will affect the social order of the tribe.

When the first-person plural is absorbed into the 'I' of leadership, the immediate response to emergencies is to put trust in a collective plan. The plan requires a goal (territory, quarry, etc.) and a strategy for achieving it together. This will be the normal mode of thought throughout the tribe, whenever food runs out or the rival threatens. There is neither time nor leisure for the invis-

77 See, for example, J. Itani, 'The Origin of Human Equality', in M. R. A. Chance, *Social Fabrics of the Mind*, London, 1988.

ible hand, and slow-forming consensual solutions will be rare and of their nature ill-adapted to the always present emergency. What to a settled and law-abiding community is the only avenue to rational decision-making will be, for the beleaguered tribe, a sure way to disaster. Hence the planning mentality will be the sum of politics, the only recourse in all matters in which collective survival is at stake.

Equally inevitable, in the circumstances, will be the habit of aggregating goods. The long-term perspective, which enables people to weigh one good against another, to choose between goods and to recognize the partial nature of all our satisfactions, will not be available. As in a war, each target achieved is an addition to the collective salvation, and the tribe will no sooner fix on something as a good to be pursued than it will be added to the shared agenda. A principle of aggregation will therefore govern all multiple choices, and what, in our circumstances, amounts to a destructive fallacy will be the normal way forward into whatever territory offers itself.

The primeval tribe has a strong conception of the necessities that govern all that it does. Its passage through this world is one of continual escape from death, disease and starvation, in which the good lies always before it and the bad behind. Inevitably the collective 'I' will adopt a one-dimensional view of its destiny, seeing itself as driven forward by forces with which it is wise to be aligned. There is a moving spirit, an inexorable fate, that governs the world, and the valid plan is the one that aligns itself with the moving spirit's will. Propitiation of this spirit will be a central feature in tribal religion, and the paradoxical belief that our decisions must also coincide with the force of destiny will be all-pervasive.

Naturally, despite these straitened circumstances, there will be room for dissent and scepticism. The tribe will contain prophets who warn against the mad stampede into the future, who try to moderate the one-dimensional thinking of the leader, and who recognize the fleetingness of the tribe's emergency-fuelled goals. All the doubts and traumas of the tribe will be hurled at these prophets. All those conflicts that have been, of necessity, suppressed, since the institutions do not exist that will enable the people to bring them into the open and resolve them, will be blamed on the prophet; he will be identified as outside the tribe, and not entitled to the benefits of membership. He will therefore provide the tribe with a valuable opportunity for guilt-free sacrifice. He has forfeited his life, and a great purging of doubt and hesitation will occur when he is killed – maybe on the altar of that god who represents the very moving spirit by which the pure intentions of the collective 'I' are guided.

Some such mechanism has been postulated by René Girard, as the source from which the sense of the sacred derives.[78] A society without settled law or the instruments of negotiation will be riven by conflicts, as powerful rivals imitate each other's appetites and

78 See René Girard, *La violence et le sacré*, Paris, 1972, and *Le bouc émissaire*, Paris, 1982.

powers. The sacrificial victim is chosen because he has set himself outside the social order: he is the one we are entitled to kill, and whose death will not initiate the cycle of revenge since we all of us converge on wanting it. But we don't need to go all the way with Girard in order to recognize the need that will certainly arise, in the conditions of enforced optimism that are the sole guarantee of the tribe's survival, for the scapegoat whose death will wash away the accumulated doubts.

My description of the primordial community is speculative and shorn of detail. But it seems to me to have the ring of truth. And it prompts a somewhat depressing conclusion, which is that the fallacies that I have identified in this book, as underlying the follies of our time, are not new additions to the repertoire of human madness but the residues of our forefathers' honest attempts to get things right. They represent thought-processes that were selected in the life-and-death struggles from which settled societies eventually emerged. Hence it is not surprising if, today, they define the default position to which thinking returns, whenever the future presses its claims on us. This is surely part of the explanation of the otherwise extraordinary fact that the outlook of unscrupulous optimists cannot be rectified by argument, that they surround themselves with impregnable defences against the truth, and commandeer whatever sphere of influence is available to them, so as to make it dangerous to question their ideas.

In the light of this, you might think that there is, after all, no use for pessimism, that the attempt to insert the precious virus of doubt into the armoured immune system of the progressive idea is bound to fail. In what follows, however, I will try to suggest that there is, in fact, cause for hope. Optimism, of the kind that I have criticized in this book, strives to defend itself against the new, post-Pleistocene realities. It is the other side of a kind of existential despair, a longing to retreat from the complexities of the great society to the primordial simplicity of the undifferentiated tribe. It expresses a kind of distrust of humanity, an inability to allow that we can actually move on from our original nature, and create a flexible, reasonable and charitable 'we', which is not a collective 'I' at all, but the by-product of individual freedom. But this distrust is unfounded. The world is, in fact, a much better place than the optimists allow: and that is why pessimism is needed.

ELEVEN

Our Civil Present

The people that walked in darkness have seen a great light:
they that dwell in the land of the shadow of death, upon them
hath the light shined.

Isaiah 9:2

Evolutionary psychologists have tried to persuade us that the clue to the human psyche is adaptation. By seeing those mysterious traits like altruism, sexual fidelity and the love of beauty as adaptations that favour the reproduction of our genes, we understand their origin and their nature, and can rest content with the conclusion that, like the other animals, we are, as Richard Dawkins puts it, 'survival machines' in the service of our genes.

I don't say that is entirely wrong. But it is deeply misleading. For it implies that the behaviour of the officer who saves his troops by throwing himself onto a live grenade is to be explained in just the same way as the behaviour of the bee at the hive, which loses its life by stinging the intruder. Everything that is distinctive of the human motive – the knowledge of death, the concern for others, the overcoming of fear, the act of self-sacrifice – is left out of account, along with the reasoning, the moral education and the social consciousness that implanted such a motive in the soul.[79] Even if the thing called altruism by the evolutionary psychologists were not an adaptation, and had disappeared from all other species, human beings would still exhibit it. They would still make sacrifices, still live for others, still obey the law of *agape*, which is implanted in them by reason and requires no biological basis to be real.

Hence human communities evolve in another way from the groups, herds and colonies of animals. They evolve as societies of rational beings, bound to each other by accountability, friendship and respect. They resolve their conflicts not only through power and intimidation, but also through negotiation, compromise and law. At a certain stage in the development of their rational capacities our ancestors ceased to wander in search of sustenance and settled down to create it. The transition from hunter-gatherer to farmer was perhaps the greatest transition that our species has ever encompassed. And, in the dim reaches of ancient records, we can still glimpse the price that our ancestors paid. God preferred the savoury gift of Abel's victim to the fruit of Cain's orchard, and in his resentment Cain slew his brother. The first murder was

79 See, for example, the account of the altruistic motive given by Matt Ridley in *The Origins of Virtue: Human Instincts and the Evolution of Cooperation*, Harmondsworth, 1996.

that committed by the farmer, who had rejected the bond of brotherhood, abjured the collective 'I' of the hunting tribe, and begun to live in another way, negotiating with his neighbours, defending his borders and tilling his patch. Murder of the brother symbolizes a primeval guilt – the guilt of the individual who has turned his back on the tribe. This was the *real* original sin. And it didn't go unpunished. Cain was driven out by God: his settling was unsettled, and God said to him, 'a fugitive and a vagabond shalt thou be in the earth' (Genesis 4:12).

At the back of this story we sense a prolonged crisis. Not just the sin of leaving the tribe, but the uncertainty of settlement, as the new race of farmers is uprooted and driven out. A new evil has entered the world, an evil unknown to the hunter-gatherer. For by owning land you risk the loss of it. The Old Testament is invaded at every point by a kind of darkness, as farms, vineyards and villages that have briefly enjoyed God's protection are one after another destroyed. And yet, through this darkness, the rays of light from time to time will penetrate. From the depths of despair into which the psalmists and the prophets so often lead us, we look up to see the shining city on the hill. The city too can be destroyed, and many and horrible are the seiges and massacres to which the Old Testament bears witness. But the city remains as a symbol – the place where settlement is permanent, law reliable and peace secure. The Babylonian exile is exile from the true city – the city that was ours, the place of refuge, and the temple to our God.

In his striking work *The Origin and Goal of History*, the philosopher Karl Jaspers describes what he calls the 'axial age': the period between 800 and 400 BCE when, simultaneously and without any apparent communication, human communities emerged from darkness into self-awareness and the feeling for liberty. The Homeric poems, the pre-Socratic philosophers, the Old Testament prophets; the Upanishads, Lao-Tzu, Confucius and the Buddha: all these belong to Jaspers's axial age and exemplify the same spiritual awakening, for which he gives a sketchy explanation in terms of the competition between small and emerging states. In all the records that Jaspers mentions we see the marks of the same transition – from wandering collectivities to free individuals, from clans and blood-brothers to law-abiding neighbours, from a life of emergencies to one of settled worship, in which the words and rituals are found to evoke the eternal, the reliable and the true. In other words, we see the transition that the evolutionary psychologists cannot accommodate, from hunter-gatherer to farmer, and from the tribal collective to the community of free individuals. This is a transition that occurred in the self-understanding of mankind, one in which our genes played only a subordinate part. Describe it, if you like, as an adaptation, but remember that this offers no explanation of how it came about – only an explanation of why it didn't go away.

The city entered the soul of mankind, and with it a new perspective on each other and on the conflicts that competition brings. The city is not a community of brothers: it is not a tribe or a clan, but a settlement, and if it divides into parts they are defined as parishes or wards, like the *contrade* that compete in the Palio of Siena, or else as trades and guilds, portrayed in festive mood by Wagner in the last act of *Die Meistersinger von Nürnberg*. The city is a community of neighbours who do not necessarily know each other, but whose obligations come from settlement. A neighbour, according to the Anglo-Saxon etymology, is one who 'builds nearby'. Citizens have settled side by side, and are bound by the many tacit and explicit agreements that they make with each other every day. The city is the symbol and realization of the new form of reasonableness that emerges when the way of the tribe is left behind.

In discussing the Austrian theory of the market I remarked on the similarity between that theory and the approach to tradition that was first made articulate in Burke's *Reflections on the French Revolution*. Both arguments depend upon the idea that rational solutions to social problems may *evolve*, and that the evolved solution will be sensitive to information concerning the needs and wants of strangers. This information will be destroyed by top-down planning, which will advance towards unpredicted and unpredictable outcomes, but without the information that might influence these outcomes for the common good. For Burke, the principal gift of tradition was the state of mind that he called 'prejudice', by which he meant a form of thought evolving from the pooled experiences of absent generations. Prejudice eschews abstract solutions and serves as a barrier against the illusion that we can make everything anew, according to some ideally rational plan. It is not irrational: on the contrary, it strikes a path towards collective reasonableness. The rational plan, by contrast, which imports a collective goal where no goal can be coherently intended, and which cannot adapt to changes in the wants and needs of individual agents, will be unreasonable in its execution, as in its aim. Planning may be the proper response to emergencies and to zero-sum conflicts, as in a war. But it cannot solve the conflicts of civil society, or provide government with a goal.

Such arguments, which provide the intellectual core of a certain kind of conservatism, are not merely moves in a political debate. They are pointing to the emergence, in historical societies, of a new kind of collective rationality – not the 'I'-rationality of a leader and his plans, but the 'we'-rationality of a consensual community. It is to this 'we' rationality that the cautious pessimist refers, when attempting to neutralize false hopes. Although, as I argued in Chapter Nine, mankind has inherited fierce and often frightening defences against those who would puncture its illusions, the underlying tendency of civilization, and indeed its defining feature, is to give those people a chance. The opening of the community to doubt and hesitation, the granting of a voice to the prophet – this is the beginning of wisdom. And from this there emerges a new kind of order, in which discovered law replaces revealed commands, negotiation replaces domination, and free exchange replaces centralized distribution according to the ruling plan. Such is the order of the city, and it is an order that combines individual freedom with a genuine first-person plural. It is vulnerable to the sudden return of the 'I'-rationality and the zero-sum frenzy of the resentful – and this we have witnessed abundantly in recent times. But it also has the ability to maintain itself in being, through the institutions and customs of a free community. It seems to me that our current confrontation with the Islamists ought to have awoken us to the fact that there is something precious at stake, and that this precious thing is precisely what has enabled us to live as a free community of strangers, without submitting to tribal intimacies and top-down commands. In conclusion, it seems right to review some of the distinctive features, both institutional and individual, that have made it possible for us to live side by side in freedom, and without investing our social feelings in the false hopes that have so often brought disaster on mankind.

The order of the city is not that of the family. It is an order of 'civil society'. It does not suppose that people can easily agree or that there is any one goal towards which they aspire. It sees people as irretrievably diverse, but possessed, nevertheless, of the capacity to live in peace and to adapt through consent and consensus. On these cautious foundations has been built the modern conception of citizenship, according to which law is made legitimate by the consent of those who must obey it. This consent is delivered by a political process through which each person participates in the making and enacting of the law. The right and duty of participation is what we mean by 'citizenship', and the distinction between political and religious communities can be summed up in the view that political communities are composed of citizens, religious communities of subjects – of those who have 'submitted' (which is the primary meaning of the word *islam*). And if we want a simple definition of civil society, it would be wise to take the concept of citizenship as our starting point. That is what the millions of migrants are roaming the world in search of: an order that confers security and freedom in exchange for consent – an order not of submission but of settlement.

The comparison with Islam is pertinent. During its declining years the Ottoman Empire made persistent efforts to import the European conception of citizenship and civil society, and with it codes of man-made law that would replace the conception of law still adhered to by the *'ulema* – the scholars and jurists of the mosques. For the *'ulema* law is a divine command, discovered from the four legitimate sources: the Koran, the *sunna*, the consensus of scholars and analogy. After the collapse of the Empire, Atatürk dethroned the *'ulema* and shaped modern Turkey as a secular state, governed by secular law. A similar approach was adopted elsewhere in the Middle East; but the Islamists have never accepted it. Their philosophy has been that of the Muslim Brotherhood, and of its chief intellectual spokesman Sayyid Qutb who, in his great commentary on the Koran[80] and in his shorter polemic, *Milestones*, argued that God's will, as revealed in the

---

80   Sayyid Qutb, *Fi Zilal al-Qur'an (In the Shade of the Koran)*, 1954 onwards.

Koran and the life of the Prophet, is the only legitimate source of law; that all forms of secular authority are illegitimate; and that the nation-state, with its purely territorial sovereignty, has no authority over those whom it claims to command.

Qutb's view attacks civil society in its very core, since it denies the basis of civil order in settlement, makes territory insignificant and construes law as a top-down command from the single source of authority: the over-arching 'I' that is the 'I' of God. It goes hand in hand with a retreat from civil society and the order of free consensus to the imperative bonding of the tribe. Hence the advocacy of brotherhood (*Ikhwan*) as the true alternative to nationality and the nation-state. The longing for brotherhood is associated with the belief that the tribe and the family are the true sources of legitimate succession – a belief that has caused the schisms from which Islam has always suffered. We should not regard the association of a divine-command view of law with tribal order and the appeal to brotherhood as merely accidental: all three involve a reversion to the hunter-gatherer community that I described in the last chapter. The conflict between Cain and Abel, the aftermath of which can be everywhere discerned in the Old Testament, is still being played out in the Koran.

The long experience of settlement encourages the view that law is not a system of commands, rained down on human society from the divine stratosphere, but rather a residue of human agreements. Law doesn't tell us what to do, but what not to do; it leaves us free to pursue our own goals, within side-constraints that express the consensus of our neighbours. Its authority does not derive from God but from man, and its jurisdiction is defined by the shared territory, and not by faith, family or tribe. Such was the conception of law that arose in the Greek *polis* and was built by the Roman jurists into a universal system.

All that ought to be evident to British and American citizens, who have enjoyed the inestimable benefit of the common law – a system that has not been laid down by some sovereign power, but built up by the courts, in their attempts to do justice in individual conflicts. Our law is a 'bottom-up' system, which addresses the sovereign in the same tone of voice that it uses to address the citizen – namely by insisting that justice, not power, will prevail. Hence it has been evident since the Middle Ages that the law, even if it depends on the sovereign to impose it, can also depose the sovereign if he tries to defy it. This feature of the common law goes hand in hand with its ability to provide creative solutions to social problems and conflicts, in a manner sensitive to the wants and needs of individuals. The common law is perhaps the most vivid example that we have of the triumph of reasonable solutions over instinctive urges.

A society of settled people is held together as much by territory as by religion, and indeed, in due time, religion may decline or fragment without damage to the rule of law. God's commandments are important, but they are not seen as sufficient for the good government of human societies: instead they are regarded as *constraints*, in the manner outlined in Chapter Six. Moral and spiritual laws govern the moral life, but they do not regulate society, which is an association of free individuals, all with purposes of their own. Moral and spiritual laws must therefore be supplemented by another kind of law, one that is responsive to the changing forms of human conflict. This was made transparently clear by Jesus in the parable of the Tribute Money ('Render unto Caesar what is Caesar's, and to God what is God's'), and by the Papal doctrine of the 'Two Swords' – the two forms of law, human and divine, on which good government depends.[81] The law enforced by our courts requires the parties to submit only to the secular jurisdiction. It treats all parties as responsible individuals, acting freely for themselves. Law exists in order to resolve conflicts among free beings, not in order to lead them to salvation.

The contrast between the order of the city and the order of the tribe therefore goes hand in hand with another, between territorial and divine jurisdiction. Civic feeling marginalizes loyalties of family, tribe and faith, and places before the citizen's mind, as the focus of patriotic sentiment, not a person or a group but a place. This place is the city and its territory, defined by the history, culture and law that have made it *ours*. Territorial loyalty is composed of land, together with the narrative of its possession. Such was the loyalty of the Greek citizen to the *polis*; and such has been the loyalty of Europeans to the land of their birth.

It is this form of territorial loyalty that has enabled people in

---

81   I have defended this position at length in *The West and the Rest*, Wilmington, DE, 2002.

Western democracies to exist side by side, respecting each other's rights as citizens, despite radical differences in faith, and without any bonds of family, kinship or long-term local custom to sustain the solidarity between them. This is the foundation of the society of strangers, living at peace with each other and managing their differences through the ways of consent. There is no chance that flawed humanity can find a better overall arrangement. Certainly the arrangement can be improved, just as it can decay; but radical alternatives invariably end by destroying the foundation of the 'we', and putting a tyrannical 'I' in its place.

In the *Muqaddimah* – the prologue to his universal history – the fourteenth-century Tunisian polymath Ibn Khaldun argued that the order of the city is essentially fragile, destined to give way under the effect of leisure and luxury, and to lose the ability to defend itself against the order of the tribe. The tribes surrounding the city are held together by *'asabiyah*, a kind of pre-political force that binds the tribe as a sinew (*'asab*) binds a limb. The city itself is held together only by the weak force of politics, itself subject to the corruption of luxury and self-interest. Ibn Khaldun's theory does not rightly comprehend the city or the nation as Westerners have known it, though it certainly contains a warning for us, here, now. And it reflects the experience of many Muslims, for whom territorial loyalty and secular jurisdiction have been fragile and provisional, and who have returned to tribal *Ikhwan* and 'the shade of the Koran' whenever the society of strangers seems too weak a form of social bonding.

This is surely what we are now seeing, not only in Pakistan and among the Wahhabists of Saudi Arabia, but also wherever the refugees from the *shari'ah* have tried to settle, carrying its vision of a transcendental community in their hearts. And it is a development that deeply concerns us. Al-Qaeda is a product of the fallacies that I have described in this book. It promises a divine plan, a top-down government and a utopian vision; and it holds up the success of others as a reason to punish them. It is aligned with the moving spirit, following an irresistible path to the goal in which all the goods promised by the Prophet will be realized together, and the world of compromise and half measures will finally be left behind.

It has been my purpose to defend that world of compromise and half measures. Many attempts have been made by utopians and planners to destroy it. But the desire for negotiated solutions, the habit of conceding to others the freedom to differ and the freedom to be, the deference to established custom – all these still exist. And they are associated with two habits that are, I believe, the long-term gifts of settlement and the spiritual legacy of our European way of life: the habits of forgiveness and irony.

Happiness does not come from the pursuit of pleasure, nor is it guaranteed by freedom. It comes from sacrifice: that is the great message that is conveyed by all the memorable works of our culture. It is the message that has been lost in the noise of false hopes, but which, it seems to me, can be heard once again if we devote our energies to retrieving it. In the Judaeo-Christian tradition the primary act of sacrifice is forgiveness. Those who forgive sacrifice resentment, and renounce thereby something that had been dear to their heart. Forgiveness means stepping down from the 'I' posture, in full deference to the 'we'. It is the standard of civilization, and the habit that makes civilization possible.

Forgiveness can be offered only on certain conditions, and a culture of forgiveness is one that implants those conditions in the heart. You can forgive those who have injured you only if they acknowledge their fault: and acknowledgement is not merely a cognitive attitude. It is not achieved by saying 'yes, that's true, that's what I did'. It requires penitence and atonement. Through these self-abasing acts the wrongdoer goes out to his victim and re-establishes the moral equality that makes forgiveness possible. In the Judaeo-Christian tradition all this is well known, and incorporated into the sacraments of the Roman Catholic Church as well as the rituals and liturgy of Yom Kippur. We have inherited from those religious sources the culture that enables us to confess to our faults, to make recompense to our victims, and to hold each other to account in all matters where our free conduct can harm those who have cause to rely on us. Accountability in public office is but one manifestation of this cultural inheritance, and we should not be surprised that it is the first thing to disappear when the utopians and the planners take over. Nor should we be surprised that it is entirely absent from the world of the Islamists

– even though forgiveness has an important place in the practice of Islam and in the morality of the Koran.[82]

From the culture of forgiveness springs the other habit that helps us to be at home in the society of strangers. This is irony, by which I mean the habit of acknowledging the otherness of everything, including oneself. However convinced you are of the rightness of your actions and the truth of your views, look on them as the actions and views of someone else, and rephrase them accordingly: such is the principle by which, in our better moments, we wish to live. As the dialogues of Plato display, irony was the defining grace of the Greek city-state. A certain cult of irony was passed on through the Roman comedy to the literature of the Middle Ages, to achieve sublime expression in the works of Chaucer and Boccaccio. Nor has irony been absent from the literature of Islam, as we know from the *Thousand and One Nights* and the laughing piety of the Sufi poets, heavily censored today in the land of their birth.

Irony is quite distinct from sarcasm: it is a mode of acceptance, rather than a mode of rejection. And it points both ways: through irony I learn to accept both the other on whom I turn my gaze, and also myself, the one who is gazing. Irony is not free from

82 See, for example, Koran, 13:22. This is not to say that the message of the Koran is identical in this respect with that contained in the Judaeo-Christian tradition. Both Jesus and Rabbi Hillel placed love and forgiveness at the centre of morality; for the Koran that central place is occupied by submission. Love and forgiveness may be *signs* of submission, but they are not what it consists in.

judgement: it simply recognizes that the one who judges is also judged, and judged by himself. And it clears the space in which a collective rationality – one that acknowledges others even while knowing nothing of their desires – can grow in the heart of things.

Forgiveness offers the opportunity to repair things, to emerge from conflict into resolution, and to silence the call to revenge. In the world of *Ikhwan* another rule prevails: 'I and my brother against my cousin; I and my cousin against the world', as the Arabic proverb has it. And from that rule comes the blood feud, the retreat into the family, and the destruction of the public square. Recent opinion polls suggest that the majority of Muslims are appalled by the conduct of the Islamists, and are as eager to find a way to live by peaceful compromises as their non-Muslim neighbours.[83] Nevertheless, the Pleistocene mindset of the Islamists is indifferent to public opinion, and has set itself the task – parallel to that adopted by the tiny band of Bolsheviks in 1917 – of entirely destroying the forms of settled government. It is drawn to terrorism not because of anything that could be achieved by it, but because terrorism is a refuge from settlement and a return to the all-commanding 'I'.

Terror is therefore not a tactic used to accomplish some negotiable goal. It is an end in itself and a source of exultation. Even if there is a goal, terror remains disconnected from it. And the

83   See www.WorldPublicOpinion.org.

goal is usually vague and utopian to the point of unreality. Its non-achievement is part of its point – a way to justify the constant renewal of violence. And terrorists might equally be causeless, or dedicated to a cause so vaguely and metaphysically character- ized that nobody (least of all themselves) could believe it to be achievable. Such were the Russian nihilists, as Dostoevsky and Turgenev described them. Such too were the Italian Brigate Rosse and the German Baader-Meinhof gang of my youth. As Michael Burleigh shows, in his magisterial study *Blood and Rage*,[84] modern terrorism has been far more interested in violence than in anything that might be achieved by it. It is typified by Joseph Conrad's Professor in *The Secret Agent*, who raises his glass 'to the destruction of all that is'.

Terrorism is thereby directly connected to the utopian fallacy. The vague or utopian character of the cause means that every- thing is permitted in pursuit of it. The cause is part of a search for meaning: it is the high point of the 'I' mentality, which sees other people as a means to self-exaltation. To kill someone who has neither offended you nor given just cause for punishment you have to believe yourself wrapped in some kind of angelic cloak of justification. You then come to see the killing as showing that you are indeed an angel. Your existence is given its final ontological proof. The exultation pursued by terrorists is, characteristically, a moral exultation, a sense of being beyond the reach of ordinary

84   Michael Burleigh, *Blood and Rage: A Cultural History of Terrorism*, London, 2008.

human judgement, radiated by a self-assumed permission of the kind enjoyed by God. Even in its most secularized form, therefore, terrorism involves a kind of religious hunger. It expresses the primeval longing for the collective 'I', living in and through emergencies, guided by the moving spirit, and with neither the need nor the ability to compromise with strangers.

Of course, terrorists are surrounded by society of another kind. They stand in the midst of a settled community. And the terrorist senses this as a reproach. It is, in a way, as difficult for him as it would be for you or me to kill the innocent Mrs Smith and her children as they go about their family shopping. Hence his *gran rifiuto* cannot begin simply from the desire to kill. Mrs Smith must become something else – a symbol of some abstract condition, a kind of incarnation of a universal enemy with which the terrorist is locked in a zero-sum conflict. Hence terrorists lean on doctrines that remove the humanity from the people they target. The target is the Great Satan, as manifest in Mrs Smith. Or else it is the class that contains her: the bourgeoisie, for example, the 'class enemy', who had the same function in Bolshevik ideology as the Jew in the ideology of the Nazis. Mrs Smith and her children stand behind the target, which is the Great Satan, the abstract bourgeois family or the World Zionist Conspiracy. It just so happens that, when the bomb hits this target made of fictions, the shrapnel passes easily through it into the real body of Mrs Smith. Sad for the Smiths, and often you will find terrorists making a kind of abstract apology, saying that it was not their fault that Mrs

Smith got clobbered, and that really people ought not to stand behind targets in quite that way.

Islamist terrorists are animated, at some level, by the same troubled search for the original unity of the tribe and the same need to stand above their victims, in a posture of transcendental exculpation. Ideas of liberty, equality or historical right have no influence on their thinking, and they are not interested in possessing the powers and privileges that their targets enjoy. The things of this world have no real value for them, and if they sometimes seem to aim at power it is only because power would enable them to establish the kingdom of God – an aim that they, like the rest of us, know to be impossible and therefore endlessly renewable in the wake of failure. Their carelessness of others' lives is matched by a carelessness towards their own. Life for them has no particular value and death beckons constantly from the near horizon of their vision. And it is in death that they perceive the only meaning that matters: the final transcendence of this world, and of the accountability to others that this world demands of us.

People of liberal sentiment find it difficult to accept that such a motive exists. They prefer to believe that all conflicts are political, concerning who has power over whom. They are apt to believe that the causes of Islamist terrorism lie in the 'social injustice' against which the terrorists are protesting, and that their regrettable methods are made necessary by the fact that all other attempts to rectify things have failed. This seems to me radically to misinterpret the motives of terrorism in general and of

Islamism in particular. The Islamist terrorist, like the European nihilist, is primarily interested in himself and his spiritual condition, and he has no real desire to change things in the surrounding settlement, where he does not belong. He wants to belong to God, not to the world, and this means witnessing to God's law and kingdom by destroying all that stands in its way, his own body included. Death is his ultimate act of submission: through death he is dissolved into a new and immortal brotherhood. The terror inflicted by his death both exalts the world of brotherhood and casts a devastating blow against the rival world of strangers, in which citizenship, not brotherhood, is the binding principle.

'The best lack all conviction, while the worst / Are full of passionate intensity.' Yeats's famous words were written in 1919, most probably in reaction to the Russian Revolution, and as part of an apocalyptic vision of the destruction to come. But they can be read in another way, as a universal truth. The transition from hunting to settlement permits the emergence of the best community that humans can hope for – a community without conviction, in which nobody believes he has the divine right or the hisorical duty to make war on those who disagree with him: a community in which irony flourishes and forgiveness has a chance. Of course, such a community does not *entirely* lack conviction. It depends on constraints, on a sense of life's meaning and on the quiet faith that maintains those things in being through hardship and strain. But it will be profundly opposed to the 'life of conviction', in which an overarching commitment obliterates the hesitations which are the best we can hope for, when addressing the long-term future of mankind.

The worst are precisely those who wish to sweep away the settled community of strangers, and to impose in its place either a divinely ordered 'brotherhood', or the conscripted unity of a society at war. The best are those who are no more convinced about anything, than they are convinced that convictions should not matter. Robespierre, Lenin, Hitler, Sartre, Mao and Bin Laden do not share many features. But they are united in one thing, which is the 'passionate intensity' that comes from demanding conviction and unity in the place of settlement and doubt.

This is why we should recognize that the confrontation that we are involved in is not political; it is not the first step towards a negotiation or a calling to account. It is an existential confrontation between the collective 'I' of belligerence and a negotiated 'we' that stands for nothing except the invisible hand of consensual politics. Seeing things in that way involves looking on our condition in another way from that of the optimist and the enthusiast. It involves trying to understand the first-person plural of which we are a part, and to make room for others in whatever we think and do. It means ceasing to live by schemes and plans, ceasing to blame others for our faults and failures, ceasing to think of ourselves as endowed with some angelic innocence that only the corruption of society prevents us from displaying and enjoying. It involves an attitude of care – care towards institutions, customs and consensual solutions. It involves a recognition that it is easier to destroy than to create, and that we fulfill our task on earth if we look after the small corner that is ours, and take that 'ours' to heart.

The contrast that I have drawn between two kinds of reasoning, one readied for emergencies, the other seeking agreement and compromise, reflects a fundamental duality in the human condition. People may unite behind a leader in pursuit of a goal, trusting for a fair share of the booty; or they may cooperate, negotiate and compromise, creating a public space in which goals diversify, goods are produced and free relations begin. In the world of commands and plans life is cheap, as it is in wartime and as it was in that primal search for territory. In the world of cooperation and compromise life is precious: it is everything to each of us, and we negotiate for its protection.

Both frames of mind are necessary to us. The fallacies that I have diagnosed in this book come about not because the thinking that they exemplify is absurd, but because it involves applying in times of peace and social cooperation the attitude of war. In emergencies we must switch from consensus to command, from freedom to submission, and from the order of the market to the order of the plan. We set aside the history of human cooperation, so as to return to the life-and-death struggle from which our world began. And because the way of compromise 'lacks all conviction' many people – young men especially – are dissatisfied with it. They seek the commitment that will absorb them and extinguish their individual goals; they yearn for the unified plan that will take away the burden of accountability, and for the zero-sum encounter with the enemy that will summon them to sacrifice. Hence, in the midst of the settled community, the longing will exist for another, more visceral, and more deeply unified order. And this longing will be expressed with a 'passionate intensity' that will be constantly tempted towards violence.

In religion too these contrasting frames of mind wrestle with each other, and we can see their conflict exemplified in the two Testaments of the Christian Bible. The Old Testament describes the aftermath of those first moves towards settlement: tribes at war, united behind warrior kings, searching for territory, and looting and killing in the name of the Lord. Prophets appear, warning against the futile hope for worldly salvation. But they are cast out, and the madness goes on, until all has been destroyed by it and nothing remains save the Lamentations of Jeremiah.

The New Testament describes a settled community, living under foreign jurisdiction, but retaining its customary and religious law. Into this community comes a prophet of a new kind – one who does not merely warn against sin and laxity, but who describes himself as the way, the truth and the life. He preaches new ways of thinking, new ways of living, without plans, commands or marching orders, but trusting all to the love of God and the love of neighbour. He advocates meekness and compassion, and tells us to ask God to forgive our trespasses, 'as we forgive those that trespass against us'. And he illustrates his message through his own stunning example, offering himself as a sacrifice and forgiving his tormentors, 'for they know not what they do'.

It is surely possible to see, in this new attitude to the religious life, a record of a great transition in social thinking, from the realm of commands, to that of free relations between people who, while having no unity of purpose, see each other as bound by the ground rules of cooperation. Judaism, Hinduism, Confucianism and Buddhism show the same evolution, and if Islam is a problem in the world today, it is surely because of its top-down, commanded approach to the moral life, and its emphasis on submission rather than forgiveness as the binding principle of society. The optimism of the Islamists, like that of the revolutionaries down the centuries, excuses every kind of destruction on the grounds of necessity and the long-term plan. It overlooks all the facts that make the long-term plan absurd and necessity a willed illusion. We should turn away from such comprehensive visions, and hold before our minds the image of human imperfection. We should recognize that whatever freedom, happiness and affection we can win for ourselves, depends upon cooperation with people as weak and self-centred as ourselves. In short, we should put true hopes in the place of false hopes, irony in the place of unity, and forgiveness in the place of submission.

TWELVE

Our Human Future

The posthumanists and the dystopians both tell us that our nature is changing. But the transhuman future that is welcomed by the one strikes alarm and apprehension in the other. The dystopians envisage futures in which some precious aspect of the human condition – freedom, friendship, love, childhood – has disappeared, leaving a bleak landscape without a trace of our known consolations. The transhumanists fight back, saying, sure, *we* could not be at home in this new world; but we won't exist there either. We will be replaced by cyborgs, designed to fit without strain into their new environment, just as we fit into ours. The transhumanists don't worry about Huxley's *Brave New World*: they don't believe that the old-fashioned virtues and emotions lamented by Huxley have much of a future in any case. The important thing, they tell us, is the promise of increasing power, increasing scope, increasing ability to vanquish the long-term enemies of mankind, such as disease, ageing, incapacity and death.

But to whom are they addressing their argument? If it is addressed to you and me, why should we consider it? Why should we be working for a future in which creatures like us won't exist, and in which human happiness as we know it will no longer be obtainable? And are those things that spilled from Pandora's box really our enemies – greater enemies, that is, than the false hope that wars with them? The civil beings whom I described in the previous chapter depend for their fulfilment upon love and friendship. Their happiness is of a piece with their freedom, and cannot be separated from the constraints that make freedom possible – real, concrete freedom, as opposed to the abstract freedom of the utopians. Everything deep in these civil beings depends upon their mortal condition, and while they can solve their problems and live in peace with their neighbours, they can do so only through the consensual 'we' that comes by compromise and sacrifice. They are not, and cannot be, the kind of posthuman cyborgs that rejoice in eternal life, if life it is. They are led by love, friendship and desire; by tenderness for young life and reverence for old. They live by the rule of forgiveness, in a world where hurts are acknowledged and faults confessed to. All their reasoning is predicated upon those basic conditions, and they will strive to retain the world that has been built from them.

The transhumanists rejoice in the future tense. But they are not so much predicting as escaping. They show the same addiction to unrealities as the unscrupulous optimists that I have been discussing in this book; and their best case scenarios are predicated on hopes as false as any entertained by the utopians. In the writings of Ray Kurzweil, Max More and Eric Drexler, we find the excited aggregation of the many things that they imagine to be good: power, scope, freedom from disease and degeneration.[85] We see the familiar *tabula rasa* vision of the human being, which tells us that we can take away the gifts of history and confront a new freedom, in which the compromises and constraints that have previously shaped us have been laid aside. There is even, I believe, a trace of the utopian fallacy in the 'predictions' of Kurzweil, whose future world, in which people are stored as information, involves radical confusions over personal identity.[86] The future of the transhumanists is urged upon us from the premise of its own impossibility.

The transhumanists might seem very far, in their thinking, from the Pleistocene tribe that I imagined in Chapter Ten. But they are in the grip of the same collective urges – urges that saw our ancestors through to the age of settlement, but which persist today only to unsettle us. The transhumanists show us a future that is 'necessary', a fate determined by the moving spirit of scientific progress. To ignore that future is not to resist it, but to

85 See Max More, 'Principles of Extropy', 1990; K. Eric Drexler, *Engines of Creation: The Coming Era of Nanotechnology*, New York, 1986.

86 See the account of personal identity in David Wiggins, *Sameness and Substance Renewed*, Cambridge, 2001, ch. 7.

devote the limited resources of our reasoning to the only things on which they can be successfully deployed, which are present realities and the people contained in them.

Rather than lose ourselves in these unreal hopes, therefore, we should reflect again on our nature as settled, negotiating creatures, and return to the task in hand, which is to look with irony and detachment on our actual condition, and to study how to live at peace with what we find.